D1483200

BFI FILM CLASSICS

....

Rob White
SERIES EDITOR

Colin MacCabe and David Meeker
SERIES CONSULTANTS

Cinema is a fragile medium. Many of the great classic films of the past now exist, if at all, in damaged or incomplete prints. Concerned about the deterioration in the physical state of our film heritage, the National Film and Television Archive, a Division of the British Film Institute, has compiled a list of 360 key films in the history of the cinema. The long-term goal of the Archive is to build a collection of perfect showprints of these films, which will then be screened regularly at the Museum of the Moving Image in London in a year-round repertory.

BFI Film Classics is a series of books commissioned to stand alongside these titles. Authors, including film critics and scholars, film-makers, novelists, historians and those distinguished in the arts, have been invited to write on a film of their choice, drawn from the Archive's list. Each volume presents the author's own insights into the chosen film, together with a brief production history and detailed credits, notes and bibliography. The numerous illustrations have been specially made from the Archive's own prints.

With new titles published each year, the BFI Film Classics series is a unique, authoritative and highly readable guide to the great films of world cinema.

Could scarcely be improved upon ... informative, intelligent, jargon-free companions.
The Observer

Cannily but elegantly packaged BFI Classics will make for a neat addition to the most discerning shelves.
New Statesman & Society

BFI FILM CLASSICS

THE PALM BEACH STORY

John Pym

bfi Publishing

First published in 1998 by the
BRITISH FILM INSTITUTE
21 Stephen Street, London W1P 2LN

The British Film Institute
is the UK national agency with
responsibility for encouraging the arts
of film and television and
conserving them in the national interest.

British Library Cataloguing-in-Publication Data
A catalogue record for this book is available from the British Library

ISBN 0–85170–671–1

Series design by
Andrew Barron & Collis Clements Associates

Typesetting by
D R Bungay Associates, Burghfield, Berks.

Printed in Great Britain by Norwich Colour Print

CONTENTS
. . . .

To
Martha Elizabeth Pym

ACKNOWLEDGMENTS

. . . .

The Sturges papers, on which most recent writers on Preston Sturges have drawn, are housed in the Department of Special Collections, the University of California at Los Angeles. Regrettably, no latter-day sausage tycoon wandered into my home in rural Kent, in the South-East of England, to offer me an 'aerio-plane' ticket to the West Coast. I've had to rely, therefore, chiefly on secondary sources for the background information contained in this monograph, notably the recent Sturges biographies by Donald Spoto and Diane Jacobs. Sandy Sturges' edition of her husband's draft autobiography and the second volume of Brian Henderson's collection of the Sturges screenplays have also been valuable. Quoted dialogue is taken from the original screenplay of *The Palm Beach Story* along with Sturges' stage directions. I have, however, amended the lines, where necessary, so that they conform with what – on the day the shots were taken – the players actually said. I am grateful, as always, in matters relating to film credits, for the guidance of Markku Salmi, officer commanding the BFI's information database.

1

. . . .

TANGOVILLE-SUR-MER

In August 1914 the French Army advanced towards the heart of Germany and the Germans wheeled through Belgium confident that Paris would soon be theirs; meanwhile, in faraway California, the Keystone Film Company released a fusillade of five new Chaplin shorts, including *The Property Man*, one of the earliest movies (if not the earliest movie) Chaplin directed himself. As the combatants on the Western Front prepared to lock horns, sixty miles west of the Franco–Belgian border, in Deauville, a tall fifteen-year-old American schoolboy named Preston Sturges was happily occupying himself as the summer manager (and sole employee) of the new seaside branch of Maison Desti, his mother's Paris-based cosmetics business.

Born of Irish ancestry in Quebec in 1871, Preston's mother Mary Dempsey had grown up in Chicago without material advantages. By 1914, however, having dispensed with three husbands, she'd migrated to Europe as the factotum of the restless American dancer Isadora Duncan. Mary Desti, as she now styled herself, was a mercurial woman with artistic aspirations whose adult life was punctuated by a number of impulsive actions, some of which, like the cosmetics enterprise, flared and burned brightly (for a while at least), thanks to the force of her personality – and the generosity of her second husband, the Chicago stockbroker Solomon Sturges, who despite their divorce bestowed money and kindness on Mary for the rest of her life.

Ilias Pasha, the father of Mary's third husband Vely Bey, had been physician to the Turkish tyrant Abdul Hamid (Abdul the Damned), and it was through him that Maison Desti came into being. After the sultan's deposition in 1909, Ilias moved to Paris to be near his son and his son's wife (and his step-grandson Preston, Solomon Sturges' adoptive son, although in fact the child of Mary's first marriage to a wastrel named Edmund Biden – who much later tried to wheedle repayment from Preston for sums he, Biden, had advanced for treatment of one of his son's childhood illnesses …), and it was there in Paris that Mary one day asked her father-in-law for advice on a facial rash. Ilias Pasha produced a cream that, he claimed, was in common use throughout the harems of Turkey. It also smoothed away wrinkles. This cream, it turned out, was no snake oil, and Mary decided forthwith that she must find a way to market the 'Secret of the Harem' – subsequently renamed Youth Lotion.

She acquired premises on rue de la Paix, as well as the back-up for a cosmetics production line, and her initial idea was to call the business Maison D'Este. (She believed herself to be a descendant of the Este family, via Mary of Modena, the devout, quick-witted and proud wife of James II of England.) The Paris branch of the high-falutin' Estes took a different view, however, and threatened a lawsuit. Maison 'Desti' got round the difficulty: and thus Mary's personality was – leaving aside her attachments to Biden, Sturges and Vely Bey – at least doubly remade.

> Glass bottles from Venice held her new scents, the Paris box manufacturer Tolmer designed containers for Desti products, and Baccarat and Lalique sold her crystal bottles and alabaster jars [Donald Spoto records]. Rouges and face powders completed her line of products, and soon the Maison Desti was doing brisk business – so brisk in fact, that in October [1912] Mary hustled Preston off to New York for a selling trip, where B. Altman and Company bought ten thousand dollars' worth of her products. Soon after, a manufacturer offered Mary a deal to distribute her cosmetics with his perfumes. She distrusted him, however, and rejected his offer – to her perpetual regret, for the man's name was Coty.[1]

In 1914 Mary struck a deal with the owner of the fashionable Paris restaurant Ciro's, who'd rented a house for the season in the new resort of Deauville in Normandy. Maison Desti was to occupy the ground floor of Ciro's building, the restaurant would operate on the first floor, and Preston, the manager of the cosmetics shop, who was then at school in Switzerland, would sleep above the restaurant, where he was to take all his meals. The little town of Deauville was then, Sturges recalled, 'the most fashionable playground in the world'.

> Billionaires were ten cents a dozen. The beach and the casino and racetrack spilled over with dukes, barons, deposed kings, maharajahs, politicians, statesmen, newspaper owners, several Rothschilds, opera stars, generals, admirals, celebrated actors, notorious actresses, vaudeville performers, gigolos [the list

continues with another eighteen types] and, kept or loose, the prettiest women in the world.[2]

It's too much to claim that what Sturges absorbed in those few months at Deauville in 1914 deeply affected his relatively brief, but hugely successful and handsomely rewarded career as a fully-fledged Hollywood writer–director, but there is, I think, something congruent and moving about Preston's experiences in the summer of 1914, a few miles from what were soon to become the battlefields of Flanders, and what he would be doing twenty-seven years later, at the very height of his creative powers, on the eve of the Japanese attack on Pearl Harbor and America's entry into the Second World War. In both the summer of 1914 and the winter of 1941–2, in the weeks when he was hammering out *The Palm Beach Story* as an employee of Paramount Pictures, Sturges lived a curiously cocooned existence: surrounded by gaiety and excess on the eve of the First World War, and recreating with adornments the idea of another millionaires' playground on the eve of the Second.

In 1914 Chaplin's 'property man' was performing his business in a vaudeville theatre 'peopled with grotesque and unreasonably temperamental artists':[3] Sturges, meanwhile, was acting as props man (as well as stage manager and leading actor) in another dramatic endeavour, the showcase theatre of Maison Desti.

> All of the beau monde – and the less beau, too – got up late in Deauville. Everybody got up late in Deauville, except me. I rose at 5:30, put on an old pair of pants and a sweater, picked up a quick cup of coffee and a croissant from Ciro's early morning cook, who was starting to build his soups, and snuck down to the shop. I dusted it, swept it out thoroughly, polished the brass, washed the windows, then hustled back upstairs and got back in bed.
>
> At 10:30, I came down again, this time officially. Wondrously decked out in white flannel trousers, brown-and-white shoes, a tan gabardine jacket with a belt in the back, and a carnation in my buttonhole, I dropped into the shop. Assuring myself, by running a suspicious finger along the shelves, that the night porter had done his work efficiently, I retired to Ciro's to enjoy an exotic breakfast.[4]

A composite photograph of Preston Sturges taken later that year in New York ('five views for a quarter') shows an assured young man in a double-breasted dinner jacket, his left hand tucked into his jacket pocket and his right hand lying on the round table at which he's seated.[5] A smile is starting to form at the corner of his mouth, his thick dark hair is brushed up from his forehead, his features are angular and slightly over-pronounced, and his carriage is naturally erect. What one doesn't gain from this immensely attractive informal study is the authority of Preston Sturges' height, but what is conveyed, unmistakably, is the sitter's debonair style and dash.

In Deauville that summer Preston had passed for nineteen, and even formed a liaison with an attractive older girl on the strength of this minor deception, until Mary, who'd come on a weekend visit, spoiled the party by commenting to the girl, 'Isn't he *big* for fifteen?' The theme of *The Palm Beach Story* – if a featherweight romantic comedy can really be said to have anything so deep-dish as a theme – is summed up by the heroine, Claudette Colbert, in a retort to her husband: 'You have no idea what a long-leggèd gal can do without doing anything.' Preston wasn't exactly that long-leggèd gal, but he had as a youth that punchy self-confidence which can, in its own way, it seems, achieve practically anything.

> As an adolescent [Sturges recalled], I only knew a few of [Deauville's] celebrities to speak to, but I knew most of them by sight, which was useful when they came into the Desti establishment. I did know Mother's friend, Jules Bache, the banker, and Maurice and Florence Walton, the great ballroom dancers, and Elsie Janis, and Bayo, the world's greatest tango dancer, and Irene Bordoni, and Tod Sloan, and Kid McCoy, and Frank Moran …
>
> The darling of all these people and the uncrowned King of Deauville was the son of an Auvergnat grocer, a tiny little man who looked like a jockey. His real name was Goursat, but under the signature of Sem he had become the world's most extraordinary caricaturist. To be ridiculed by Sem was a great honor. His albums of drawings, beginning with *Tangoville-sur-Mer*, which celebrated the heyday of Deauville, are collectors' items and perfectly remarkable. Everybody who was anybody is there, instantly recognizable and hilariously drawn. It is difficult to

prove how truly phenomenal he was because caricature is an evanescent pursuit, the one form of portraiture which demands of the viewer complete familiarity with the features of the victims. With the passage of time, their faces are nearly always forgotten. Sem was by far the greatest talent in this anteroom of the arts I have ever seen during my lifetime.[6]

Sturges himself was to become something more than a caricaturist – something more than a Chaplin or a Sem – but underlying many of his characters, all the characters indeed of *The Palm Beach Story*, with the exception of the two principals, are the exact lines of fluid caricature. Preston's buried caricatures have not, however, suffered the fate of the once-living subjects of Sem's sketches, or the somehow unknowable figures, swathed in pathos, of Chaplin's gallery. His great rush of comic characters have not dwindled over the years; on the contrary they have if anything become more desperately and more recognisably alive.

2
. . . .
THE PALM BEACH STORY

Two years before Preston spent his happy summer in Deauville, Adolph Zukor, a Hungarian émigré to the United States, who'd prospered in the New York and Chicago fur trade (he invented a new type of neck clasp), and then in the penny arcades of Philadelphia and Boston, founded the Engadine corporation to introduce imported films to American audiences. His first picture was *Queen Elizabeth* (*Les Amours de la Reine Elisabeth*, 1912, directed by Louis Mercanton), with the legendary but by then 60-year-old Sarah Bernhardt. On the back of this success, Zukor developed a film production company featuring 'Famous Players in Famous Plays'. Thirty years later, after the customary mergers, acquisitions and vicissitudes of Hollywood, Famous Players had become Paramount Pictures, one of the industry's 'big seven' individually distinctive studios.

Paramount established its reputation in the 1920s, having on its books such stars as John Barrymore and Rudolph Valentino; Pola Negri, Clara Bow and Douglas Fairbanks. Cecil B. DeMille's parti-coloured version of *The Ten Commandments* (1923) was the greatest of

Paramount's silent money-makers. The transition to sound caused a dip in the studio's upward progress, but by the mid-30s, when a shadow began to fall across civilised life in Europe, an influx of outstanding talent from Germany and Austria (notably Josef von Sternberg, Ernst Lubitsch and Billy Wilder) helped to consolidate Paramount's style and fortunes. The catchphrase 'Paris Paramount' – and all that implied in terms of lightness of touch and continental sophistication – suggested that the mythical studio re-creation was somehow more authentic, beautiful and perhaps, to American eyes, more appealing than Paris, France. Gary Cooper and Ray Milland as well as the more down-to-earth and bigger-than-life stars Mae West and W. C. Fields set Paramount's tone, together with those beautiful no-nonsense women Jean Arthur and Claudette Colbert.

The Palm Beach Story (first titled 'Is Marriage Necessary?' and later 'Is That Bad?') was written by Preston Sturges in two consecutive drafts between the beginning of September and the end of November 1941. From 1937 to '42, Sturges – who had found his way to California via success as a Broadway playwright – employed as secretary a well-educated young man named Edwin Gillette, and it was Preston's habit to call Gillette, often late at night, to take down the dialogue of his scripts as he paced about, playing all the parts. The second version of the screenplay, which corresponds to the completed film in most particulars, is dated 21 November – three days before shooting began on Stage Seven at Paramount studios. The budget was nearly a million dollars: the two stars with their names above the title, Claudette Colbert and Joel McCrea, receiving $150,000 and $60,000 respectively.

The film turned out to be the fifth in the run of eight movies which Preston wrote and directed for Paramount between 1940 and 1946. *The Great McGinty*, *Christmas in July* (both 1940), *The Lady Eve* (1941) and *Sullivan's Travels* (1942) preceded it; and *The Miracle of Morgan's Creek*, *Hail the Conquering Hero* (both 1944) and *The Great Moment* (1946) followed. *Sullivan's Travels*, the serio-comic story of a Hollywood director (Joel McCrea) who is fed up with making comedies and determined to find out what poverty is really like, opened in London on 2 January 1942, while *The Palm Beach Story* was still in production. Twelve days later Sturges threw an immense party for the opening of a new floor at his loss-making restaurant, The Players, on Sunset Boulevard.

No producer is listed for *The Palm Beach Story* (as was customary at Paramount during this period), although Paul Jones is credited as associate producer, the role he'd fulfilled on Preston's four previous pictures. The art director Hans Dreier and his colleague Ernst Fegté, both highly experienced German-born designers, were slated to work on the production – which did not, incidentally, for all the joviality of its content, enjoy a particularly happy passage. Dreier, like Jones, had worked on all the earlier films Sturges had written and directed, and he and Fegté had created the interior of the millionaire's mansion and the staterooms on board the ocean-going liner in *The Lady Eve*; sets which, in tone and dressing, were not unlike those required for *The Palm Beach Story*. The cameraman was Victor Milner, who had worked on several Lubitsch pictures and won an Oscar for his photography of DeMille's *Cleopatra* (1934) starring Claudette Colbert, and who'd later – like Jones, Dreier, Fegté, and the editor of *The Palm Beach Story*, Stuart Gilmore – collaborated so effectively with Preston on *The Lady Eve*.

Just before Sturges began work on the screenplay of *The Palm Beach Story*, Paramount released a nine-minute training film ('Safeguarding Military Information') on which Sturges had acted as

Preston Sturges, Claudette Colbert and the Ale and Quail Club

unpaid advisor for the Army Signal Corps early in 1941. To return for a moment to 1914: at the outbreak of the First World War, Mary Desti extricated her son from Deauville, where he'd been managing her perfume shop, romancing, and cultivating his palate at Ciro's restaurant, and shipped him back to the United States. When America joined the war in April 1917, Sturges, who was then eighteen, at once volunteered for service in the Aviation Section of the Signal Corps, but was rejected due to a blind spot in one eye. However, Mary interceded with a general she knew in Washington, and Preston was subsequently accepted as a Signal Corps cadet. After a stint at Fort Dick, Dallas, and later at the School of Military Aeronautics at Austin, Texas, Sturges went on to advanced flight training near Memphis, Tennessee. He received a reserve commission, but the war ended before he could be posted back to France.

By 1942, Preston was forty-three, and, after finishing *The Palm Beach Story*, he cited an arm injury and an 'athletic heart', among other reasons, in his successful application for exemption from active service. Apart from the training film, Sturges appears to have taken no direct part in the 40s war effort. He had no desire, for instance, to become a front-line documentarist like Frank Capra or his friend William Wyler. The script Sturges wrote in the months immediately before Pearl Harbor, and the film taken from it, *The Palm Beach Story*, which he completed in the month after the Japanese attack, is set specifically in 1942, the year in which the movie would be released (thus giving it an up-to-the-minute flavour on its first run). There is no indication, however, that the film's locations, Manhattan and Palm Beach, are the real Manhattan or Palm Beach of 1942, or any clear indication that they are in any way part of the contemporary wider world.

The film contains only one topical reference, a half-hearted and barely audible swipe at President Roosevelt, whose liberal (financial) policies Sturges disliked and felt would do permanent damage to the United States. 'Nothing is permanent in this world,' says the fabulously wealthy Princess Centimillia, 'except Roosevelt.' There are ghostly references to the war, which we will come to later, but they're so ghostly – or perhaps one should say, subliminal – as to be almost undetectable. Sturges returned to the subject of the war, or rather, more subtly, the expectations loaded on the shoulders of a young man by a small town (if not a whole country) gripped by jingoism, in *Hail the Conquering Hero*, in which a naive youngster (Eddie Bracken), the son of a First World War hero, is invalided out of the Marine Corps because of his hay fever, and who then has to avoid what he thinks will be the disappointment of the folks back home. Whatever Sturges may have felt privately about the necessity of defeating Hitler and the Japanese, it is clear that as an artist he was chiefly alive to possibilities of making entertainment not by contributing to the raft of Hollywood 'propaganda' films, but by turning propaganda (and what sprang from it) upside down.

An immense amount has been written down the years about Sturges and the body of his film work, an extraordinary (and extraordinarily eccentric) but essentially closed and fundamentally unclassifiable crazy salad. In no particular order, the movies include a faultlessly sophisticated comedy about a wealthy 'snakeologist' who's lassoed by a conscience-stricken con-woman (*The Lady Eve*); a very odd biopic about W. T. G. Morton (Joel McCrea), the Boston dentist who discovered the anaesthetic properties of ether in 1846 (*The Great Moment*); a bone-dry political satire about a tramp who becomes a state governor (*The Great McGinty*); a curiously touching, absolutely breakneck wartime farce (possibly Sturges' most unrelievedly funny film – one emerges from it in physical pain) about a girl called Trudy Kockenlocker who mislays a husband of one night called Ratzkywatzky and subsequently gives birth to sextuplets (*The Miracle of Morgan's Creek*); a bizarre adaptation of Pierre Daninos' *Les Carnets du Major Thompson* with Jack Buchanan and Martine Carol … not to mention *The Sin of Harold Diddlebock* (1946) and *The Beautiful Blonde from Bashful Bend* (1949).

The critic James Agee once took it upon himself actually to psychoanalyse Sturges in print (*Time*, 14 February 1944), but to no avail. The author Evan Connell once observed that with most writers you can see almost immediately *how it's done*. He excepted Chekhov, who, he said, kept his secrets to himself: you absolutely could not see how he did it. The same (or something similar) can, I believe, be said of Preston Sturges. The best of the films, on one level as accessible as *The Cherry Orchard* or *Uncle Vanya*, somehow fit no pattern, elude every attempt to pin them down, adhere to no philosophy – except perhaps, sometimes, to underline the truth that the world is ruled by unreason. They are, by turns, heartless, sentimental, tender and knowing. Dialogue, Sturges said disingenuously, was a matter of finding two lines that matched:

directors were 'princes of the blood', whereas the writer was merely a 'piano-mover' – well, believe that, if you must.

The Palm Beach Story was composed in eight sequences (marked 'A' to 'H') which divide roughly speaking into three parts. The first part takes place in Manhattan, in a duplex apartment (at a fictional address, which is nevertheless clearly numbered: 968 Park Avenue) and at Pennsylvania Station ('33rd Street', reads a large plaque); the second part begins on a modern streamliner train which takes two of the leading characters to Jacksonville, Florida – here they visit a smart department store and then board a yacht for Palm Beach; the third part is set chiefly in the 'enormous house' of a Palm Beach millionairess. All these locations are literally signposted, and Sturges shades in minor geographical references too, letting the audience know, for instance, that the hunting club on the train is bound for Savannah, Georgia, the stop before Jacksonville, and that the train conductor has disembarked at his hometown of Rawley, and the huntsmen's private carriage is uncoupled and left at a siding at Rockingham Hamlet.

Yet these illusory settings are specific only in so far as they anchor a precise but volatile plot – in essence they're airily imprecise, as imprecise in fact as that famous fairytale city Paris Paramount. The film's editing and post-production took place in the month the Japanese captured Manila and laid siege to Singapore, and the film was finally completed within days of the conference on the shore of the Wannsee, near Berlin, on 20 January 1942, at which Reinhard Heydrich, 'Plenipotentiary for the Preparation for the Final Solution of the European Jewish Question', addressed senior German civil servants on the practical implementation of what was to become the Holocaust.[7] *The Palm Beach Story* had its premiere in London in the summer of 1942, as the Eighth Army was preparing for what was to be its decisive battle with Rommel's Afrika Korps. 'It may almost be said,' Churchill remarked: 'Before Alamein we never had a victory. After Alamein we never had a defeat.'

PART ONE
Sequence A
In a credit montage, a young woman in a wedding gown, who appears to have gagged, tied up, and imprisoned her twin sister in a closet, hastens frantically to church. The groom, breathless and dishevelled, is waiting for her, but he too seems to have been up to no good. A caption

reads, 'and they lived happily ever after … or did they?', the music jars
to a halt, and the years flash forward from 1937 to 1942. A Park Avenue
building manager shows a Texan couple a duplex apartment which has
come up for rent due to the 'delinquency' of its present tenants. The
elderly husband, who is deaf but has a sharp line in repartee, wanders off
and encounters a young woman, Gerry Jeffers (Claudette Colbert),
dressed in her wrap and hiding behind the shower curtain in the upstairs
bathroom. Having identified himself as 'The Wienie King' (the inventor
of a Texas sausage), the elderly gentleman swiftly establishes that Gerry
is penniless, and then, partly to one-up his wife, presses seven hundred
dollars on her. Gerry phones her husband Tom (Joel McCrea) breaking
in to his sales pitch to a prospective investor. Tom, another inventor,
although an unsuccessful one, wants to build a modest working model
for a futuristic new city airport suspended on mesh cables in the sky. The
prototype, on a greenfield site, will cost ninety-nine thousand dollars.

Sequence B
Tom returns home and learns from the doorman Mike that there's no
need for him to avoid the building manager: an old man gave his wife
money to pay the rent. The jealous Tom and the indignant Gerry are, it
seems, on the verge of separation; nevertheless, Tom allows himself to
be taken to dinner by Gerry with what remains of the seven hundred
dollars after all the bills have been paid (and she has bought a new dress).
At the restaurant, Gerry suggests that she and Tom would be better
suited as brother and sister: her new suitors would, of course, have to be
in Tom's good graces, and then they'd offer him partnerships … Back
home, it is clear that Tom and Gerry are still fond of each other, despite
themselves, and Gerry allows herself to be carried upstairs to bed.

PART TWO
Sequence C
Next morning Gerry leaves Tom to seek a divorce. A cabby
recommends Palm Beach over Reno: 'This time of year … you got the
track … you got the ocean … you got palm trees … three months …
you leave from Penn Station.' Tom pursues Gerry to the station but fails
to stop her boarding a train for Florida as the guest (and mascot) of a
party of huntsmen, the Ale and Quail Club. These elderly millionaires
are well known to the train's conductor and his staff.

The huntsmen's hi-jinks leave Colbert without her clothes

Sequence D

That evening, the Wienie King, who has moved in down the hall from the Jeffers, calls to 'see that pretty girl with the nice figger', but hearing of Tom's plight gives him the air fare to Palm Beach ('… meet her with a bowkay of roses … and bring her home'). Meanwhile, on the train, the hunters are dancing merrily in their private carriage. Gerry, having done the round of the dance floor, borrows a pair of oversize pyjamas from the egregious Mr Hinch, the one sober huntsman, and retires thankfully to bed. Left behind in the bar, while their fellows ('those sissies') serenade Gerry, two Ale and Quailers begin 'trap-shooting' with live shells. Soon a full-scale shoot-up is in progress only to be halted by the grave news that Gerry has disappeared – or, rather, fled. A posse with dogs is organised. While trying to climb into an empty upper bunk in the first public carriage she comes to, Gerry makes the acquaintance of a polite young man (Rudy Vallee), in the process breaking two pairs of his pince-nez. The hounds clamber over the young man. The conductor and his men appear and the huntsmen are sent back to their private carriage which is uncoupled and left behind.

Sequence E

Next morning, Gerry learns that her clothes and her few remaining possessions have been abandoned by the rail company, along with the Ale and Quail Club. The young man of the previous night comes to her rescue and arranges a whip-round among the lady passengers. Attired in a becoming improvised ensemble (spoilt only by the word 'Pullman' across her backside), Gerry breakfasts with the young man who offers to buy her a new outfit in Jacksonville. The young man insists that Gerry cannot accept a rail ticket from him, a complete stranger, but to get round this nicely, he suggests that she should join him as a guest on his yacht for the last leg of the journey to Palm Beach. At the department store, the young man buys Gerry not a single outfit but a whole trousseau, plus an immense ruby bracelet. On the cruise down the Florida coast, the young man identifies himself as the millionaire John D. Hackensacker III, and explains that he hopes one day to marry and produce an heir. Gerry explains that once she is divorced she intends to look for a man who won't mind parting with the ninety-nine thousand dollars her husband just happens to need, and which she insists he is entitled to as compensation for having provided for her … It's clear that John D. sees himself as Gerry's knight in shining armour.

Part Three
Sequence F
When the yacht docks at West Palm Beach, John D. introduces Gerry to his assertive sister Maude, the much-married Princess Centimillia, and her current companion Toto, origin unknown, possibly Baluchistan. As the party approaches the jetty by launch, Gerry is horrified to see Tom, roses in hand, waiting to greet her. Gerry introduces Tom as her brother, 'Captain McGlue', and Tom, too bemused to do otherwise, goes along with the deception. The Princess, meanwhile, sees him as a more manly (and American) proposition than the effete Toto. Tom and Gerry are both to stay in the Princess's mansion.

Sequence G
John D. (nickname 'Snoodles') confesses to his sister that he'd like to marry Gerry, once she's free, but first he wishes to get to know her – see how she is 'when the servants leave in a body', and how she is with children. (Perhaps he could rent some children.) Meanwhile Gerry and Captain McGlue are installed in a two-bedroom suite with an intervening sitting-room. He's still jealous, and she's still determined to divorce him – and marry John D. – but

for the time being she promises that no impropriety will occur. Gerry places a Staffordshire figurine on the mantelpiece: while it remains there, she proposes, neither she nor Tom need worry about the other's fidelity. Enter John D. who opens negotiations for Gerry's hand with Captain McGlue. Enter the Princess in hysterics over her brother's plans for a mock marriage ('The boy wants to bundle!'). She exits with Tom, leaving John D. to go down on his knee to Gerry with a declaration of love. At a dinner dance at the Everglades Club, Gerry tells John D. of her *brother's* scheme to build a revolutionary new airport and he agrees to help; the Princess, however, tells Tom about John D.'s intention to buy off Gerry's husband. Tom tries to skewer Gerry's scheme to help him by informing John D. that he, Captain McGlue, is in fact a partner with Gerry's husband in the airport scheme. However, John D. sees this as no impediment (quite the reverse, in fact): he can pay Gerry's husband the ninety-nine thousand dollars he's demanding … and that money can then be used as an investment in the airport. Later that evening, as Tom and Gerry prepare for bed (he's smashed the figurine in sheer frustration), John D.'s voice serenades Gerry from the garden with full orchestral backing ('Goodnight, Sweetheart'). This is too much for husband and wife: they fall into each other's arms with Gerry observing ruefully that this is costing them millions.

Sequence H
Next morning, John D. and the Princess come upon Tom and Gerry packing their bags. The truth emerges, but despite this John D. declares he will not renege on his agreement to finance the airport. As luck will have it (it's now revealed) Tom and Gerry are both identical twins – and thus John D. will get his heir and the Princess her new husband.

3
. . . .
RICH MILLIONAIRES

Not counting the Wife of the Wienie King (who may be one), there are fourteen bona fide millionaires in *The Palm Beach Story*: John D. Hackensacker III (Rudy Vallee), 'one of the richest men in the world'; his sister Maude, the Princess Centimillia (Mary Astor), who is rich in her own right (it is to her 'enormous house' in Palm Beach that Tom and Gerry are invited) – and who has presumably married yet more (old

Italian) money; the Wienie King (Robert Dudley), who carries in his trouser pocket not so much a roll as a yule-log of hundred dollar bills; the five named members of the Ale and Quail Club, Mr Hinch (Robert Warwick), Mr Osmond the hiccuping President (Arthur Stuart Hull), Dr Kluck (Torben Meyer – 'Dr Kuck' in the screenplay), Mr Asweld the diminutive pianist (Jimmy Conlin), and Mr McKeewie (Victor Potel); as well as six others, who are unnamed on the end credit list, though they do identify themselves to the gateman at Penn Station – that noble roll call: William Demarest, Jack Norton, Rosco Ates, Dewey Robinson, Chester Conklin and Sheldon Jett. (The large somnolent Robert Greig is credited as the Third Member, but he is in fact Mr Hinch's valet.) The members of the Ale and Quail Club contained a number of the stock players who populated the background, and sometimes the foreground of several Sturges' movies: a sort of standing comic platoon – instantly recognisable, with every man in his humour.

This is not the place to enumerate Preston Sturges' many contacts with the very rich (as a baby, it is said, he was spoon-fed champagne by Isadora Duncan's mother to help him get over pneumonia) or the numerous occasions on which his mother Mary Desti was rescued by subventions from her wealthy friends; and readers who wish to know more about this aspect of Sturges' life are referred to the two biographies listed in the bibliography.

The Palm Beach Story is fantastical fiction; an unpredictable comedy peppered with whimsical inventiveness. That said, John D. Hackensacker III is of course a transparent (and not wholly unkind) parody of John D. Rockefeller III, the grandson of the oil billionaire – and, if anyone misses the point, the Hackensacker yacht, built for John D. III's grandfather, is named 'The Erl King' (say it in Brooklynese). Why 'Hackensacker'? Well, apart from the obvious alliterative echoes, Hackensack, N.J., was associated in Sturges' mind with a brief, idyllic (if somewhat unproductive) period in the 1930s when he was living near Peekskill, N.Y., just across the stateline from Hackensack, with his first wife Estelle Mudge.

Eight years before his death in 1939, *Who's Who* noted with uncharacteristic awe that John D. Rockefeller I had given 'for philanthropic and charitable purposes up to 1922 more than 500,000,000 dollars; nearly four-fifths of [which] has gone to the four great charitable corporations which he has created: the Rockefeller Foundation, General

Education Board, the Laura Spelman Rockefeller Memorial and the Rockefeller Institute for Medical Research'. JDR's grandson was a Lieutenant-Commander in the USNR and worked with the State-War-Navy Coordinating Committee from 1942 to 1945 – not quite such a milksop as yacht captain John D. Hackensacker III.

However, two wealthy individuals had a particular and more personal bearing on *The Palm Beach Story*. The first was Preston's adoptive father, the successful Chicago stockbroker Solomon Sturges, not a millionaire in the Rockefeller league, but certainly extremely wealthy, and above all 'established' in a way that neither Preston, who earned his living by his wits, nor Mary, who earned hers principally by trusting in fate, ever were. Solomon, who was born in 1865, was himself the son of a prosperous Chicago stockbroker, and took a degree at the Massachusetts Institute of Technology in 1887. Next to his mother, whose ashes Preston was said at one period to have kept in his bedroom, the person to whom Sturges remained most consistently anchored throughout his life was his rock-solid father. Solomon gave Preston money, offered him advice, stayed on good terms with his ex-wives, was not above scolding him, corresponded with him, and protected his mother. In January 1939, Solomon Sturges retired, quit Chicago, and moved to California to be near his only son. He had been in poor health for several years.

> He was just a darling, dear man [according to Priscilla Woolfan, a close friend of Sturges], and Preston obviously loved him enormously. He was so proud of him, and when Solomon felt better, Preston took him to the studio, showing him off devotedly to everyone. He spoke of his biological father as just that, his 'biological father', but when he said 'my father' he meant Solomon Sturges, whom he adored.[8]

Solomon Sturges died in April 1940, and Preston's first child, Solomon 'Mon' Sturges IV, was born in June the following year. Two months after Mon's birth, his father began to make notes for what was to become *The Palm Beach Story*. What thoughts were uppermost in Preston's mind then? It's impossible to know, but given the fourteen open-handed millionaires, all but one of whom could easily have been grandfathers – and given, too, John D.'s final act of magnanimity in agreeing to finance

Tom's airport *before* he discovers that Gerry has a twin sister – it is not, I believe, stretching speculation too far to suggest that *The Palm Beach Story* is in a sense Sturges' tribute to his father. None of the fourteen millionaires bears the slightest resemblance to Solomon, but they are all generous, and none asks anything in return – except John D. Hackensacker III who hopes that Gerry will marry him and give him an heir, John D. IV.

The other wealthy individual who had some bearing on *The Palm Beach Story*, although to a lesser if more obvious extent than Solomon Sturges, was Preston's second wife, the cereal heiress Eleanor Hutton, daughter of Marjorie Post and Edward Close, who had taken the name of her mother's second husband, the self-made financier E. F. Hutton. Sturges recalled that in 1930 he 'fell in love with a beautiful blonde' (Eleanor) on a train travelling south to Palm Beach. 'She was straight of limb, with a high-bridged nose, a clear forehead, and a sense of humour.' Preston, who was then thirty-one, was riding high as a Broadway playwright, and Eleanor, a twenty-year-old debutante, was on her way to 'Mar-a-Lago, a little seventy-bedroom cottage on the sea her mother had built a few years earlier'.[9] Donald Spoto maintains that Sturges first

encountered Eleanor at a formal dinner in Palm Beach in 1929;[10] and Eleanor herself that she met her future husband at a Park Avenue party.[11] In any event, wherever or however they met, a swift courtship followed, including 'repeated train journeys between New York and Palm Beach' (Spoto), and an offer of marriage.

> I presented myself to Mr Hutton to ask formally for Eleanor's hand in marriage. He asked if I were prepared to support the girl in the style to which she was accustomed. I told him that I had proved I could earn my living as a writer, that I had two plays then running on Broadway and that one of them alone [*Strictly Dishonorable*] brought in fifteen hundred dollars a week. 'That's pin money to her,' Mr Hutton said.[12]

Sturges' screenplay for *The Power and the Glory* (directed by William K. Howard in 1933) was based on the life of C. W. Post, Eleanor's maternal grandfather, who rose from humble origins to become an immensely successful businessman – but, 'miserable in his personal life', he committed suicide at the height of his achievements.[13] 'For Preston Sturges – and this is the central point the film makes – money was only a means to an end; as a goal in itself it was incomprehensible.'[14] Preston's marriage to Eleanor did not last. However, as Sturges later observed laconically, in one of only four references to *The Palm Beach Story* in the edited version of his memoirs, the few weeks he spent as Eleanor's house guest at Mar-a-Lago 'were not unuseful to the story'. 'Millionaires are funny,' he added.

. . . .

The first millionaire in *The Palm Beach Story*, the Wienie King, is not exactly a portrait of Sturges' one-time father-in-law, the stylish Ed Hutton, who founded with Marjorie Post what was to become the mighty General Foods, but Preston did perhaps have Mr Hutton at the back of his mind when he made the Wienie King – a decidedly unstylish elderly party – a sausage millionaire. The Wienie King invented the 'Texas Wienie', which he advises Gerry not to eat ('Lay off 'em, you'll live longer'). 'It's a good business [the sausage business],' he tells Tom, before giving him the air fare to Palm Beach, 'if you know where to buy the meat cheap. That's my secret but I ain't tellin' nobody …'

The Wienie King, when we first meet him, is dressed in a long tweed overcoat, a matching three-piece suit and an incongruous black stetson, all of which give the impression of being just slightly too large for him. He has round pebble spectacles. These accentuate his wide-awake look which acts as a sort of counterweight to his partial deafness. He would have made an ideal tortoise-like subject for the caricaturist Sem, or Ronald Searle in his American period. He is used to people shouting at him, so his policy is to shout back, louder in his high slightly other-worldly voice, without pausing for breath until he's finished what he has to say.

He's extremely quick on the uptake, not cowed by anybody; he has a ready answer, is given to aphoristic asides, and usually gets the wrong end of the stick, except when it's something important. He speaks at other people with peremptory directness and this causes exasperation. But he is impossible to ignore and, like a hyperactive two-year-old, he's liable to wander off and disappear when his mother isn't watching.

His opening sequence, when he inspects Tom and Gerry's apartment with his wife and Franklin Pangborn's prissy building manager (Pangborn was another member of the Sturges' stock company), achieves the near-impossible: it tops the baffling, but

'She's leaving the first thing in the morning'

somehow utterly exhilarating, freeze-frame credit sequence (which is driven along by a hectic higgledy-piggledy medley of the 'Wedding March' and the 'William Tell Overture'), by pitching straight into the action, by the agility of the three-way exchange, and the economy with which it establishes plot and theme.

AN ELEVATOR DOOR OPENING

From it emerges a sour-looking apartment house manager and the Wienie King and his wife. The CAMERA TRUCKS AHEAD OF THEM as they move down the hall.

THE WIFE. [We just want it as a little roost] … in case we miss the train or something … We have the big place in Yonkers.

THE MANAGER. Of course.

THE WIENIE KING. What did he say?

THE WIFE (*hollering*). He said, 'Of course.' (*Then to the Manager*) We're from Texas originally.

THE MANAGER. Of course.

THE WIENIE KING. What did he say?

THE WIFE. He said, 'Of course.'

THE WIENIE KING. Why does he keep saying the same thing all the time?

THE WIFE (*apologetically*). My husband is a little deaf.

THE MANAGER. Of course.

THE WIENIE KING. What did he say?

THE WIFE. He said, 'It's as quiet as a tomb here' … Just what we're looking for.

THE HUSBAND. I don't mind a little life … We'll be dead soon enough.

(*He pounds on a wall with his cane*) [The set sounds hollow thus making the next two lines that much funnier. JP]

A DISTANT VOICE. Come in.

THE WIENIE KING. Concrete.

AN ANGRY HEAD (*popping out from a door behind them*). I said, Come in!

THE WIENIE KING. I'm fine, thanks, how are you?

THE WIFE. I hope all the tenants aren't as disagreeable.

THE MANAGER. I can assure you they're not. The building is friendly, efficient and quiet.

(*The voice of a lady opera singer does a piercing arpeggio*)

THE MANAGER. She got in by mistake. But she's leaving the first thing in the morning.

THE WIENIE KING. What?

THE MANAGER (*cupping his hands*). I said, She's leaving the first thing in the morning.

THE WIENIE KING. Who, my wife? … You going home to see your mother?

After this lightning warm-up – which fixes the origins of the Wienie King; hints that he is not yet ready for the grave (an intro for his subsequent gift to a beautiful young woman); establishes how the Wienie King and his wife are to get back into the apartment building later in the story (they take the opera singer's apartment); reveals the Wife's bossy forwardness, which is another reason why the Wienie King gives Gerry the rent money ('This one will be a hot one on my wife. She's down there … pokin' her snoot in other people's business with that varmint eggin' her on …') – comes one of the film's most engagingly nutty sequences as the Wienie King wanders upstairs and makes a thorough

inspection of Gerry's private quarters. He rummages among the cosmetics on her dressing-table, squirting perfume and thoughtfully smelling, then licking the toothpaste. Ah! Sturges seems to be saying, the accoutrements of youth and beauty – and here he is, a deaf old man with thick glasses and no teeth, who feels the cold indoors, who has made an enormous profit – from what? Numberless unpalatable sausages. Who would want the keys to this particular kingdom?

And yet the Wienie King is far from a dry old stick: he is zestful, self-aware, direct – one of kind. Gerry, who has been hiding behind the shower curtain, can finally take no more and reveals herself in mock exasperation. The Wienie King immediately goes on the offensive: 'Hello ... What are you doing in the bathtub with your wrapper on?', then gets down to brass tacks: 'I don't suppose you go with the flat ... I guess that would be too much to hope for.' They retire to the bedroom

> THE WIENIE KING. You have a lovely clear voice ... like a bell. If I was married to you I'd hear everything you said, almost ... but you wouldn't enjoy it ... besides, I'm already married.
> GERRY (*laughing*). So am I.
> THE WIENIE KING. Me too ... Anyway I'd be too old for you ... cold are the hands of time that creep along relentlessly destroying slowly but without pity that which yesterday was young. Alone our memories resist this disintegration and grow more lovely with the passing years ... hhn, that's hard to say with false teeth. [Sturges may have called writers 'piano-movers', but one of his most distinctive and attractive skills as a screenwriter was to integrate colloquial dialogue with formal and sometimes rather beautiful 'literary' turns of phrase – as here.]

Why does the Wienie King give Gerry the rent money? Partly to best his wife, to be sure, but partly because he simply has a mind to. He likes the look of Gerry in her pink wrap. He likes birds, and there just happens to be a bird embroidered on the wrap. He knows what it is like to be poor. *He just does it.* It's in his nature. Gerry may be long-leggèd, and in the screenplay the Wienie King compliments her on her legs in an innocent old-fashioned way as she steps from the bath (a line cut from the film), but it's what she says, and the tone in which she says it, just as much as how she looks, that makes the old feller feel young again – and it's that combination of looks and attitude which is truly worth a million (or certainly a mere seven hundred dollars). Gerry gives the Wienie King a kiss on the cheek. 'Yippee! … Hot diggety!' he cries, and departs with a gleeful wave of his stick.

. . . .

After paying the rent and all the household bills, and after she and Tom have had their tipsy night out on the town, Gerry again finds herself penniless. She persuades a cabby to take her to Pennsylvania Station for free, and there she is at the gate of the platform for the noon Florida Special, waiting for something to turn up. What turns up is the Ale and Quail Club. The theme of *The Palm Beach Story* may very well be a working through of Gerry's observation 'You've no idea what a long-leggèd gal can do without doing anything', and it may even have something to do with what Sturges termed his 'theory of the aristocracy of beauty', but what audiences remember (and will always remember) first and foremost as they come out of the theatre after watching the movie, and what they cherish from the film (apart, that is, from the Wienie King eating the toothpaste, and Toto's ridiculous 'Nitzes' and 'Yitzes', and John D. ordering a prairie oyster for breakfast, 'Whatever that may be' … and any number of other felicities) is the sustained anarchy, the eruption of joyful destructiveness, the sheer childish 'clubmanship', and the handsome, howling, straining dogs of the Ale and Quail Club.

As Gerry waits by the gate, glancing at the station clock as it edges towards twelve o'clock, twelve huntsmen file past, each enquiring in a gentlemanly fashion if 'anything's the matter'. Having heard her plight, they huddle on the platform. 'You'd think one of them would *offer* a lady a ticket,' the gateman says. 'Oh … but I couldn't accept it,' Gerry replies, shocked. 'Why not … *rich millionaires* …' And so it's arranged: the Club takes a vote, Gerry is to be their guest and mascot. They have a private car and 'a ton of tickets'. They don't actually trouble to *buy* another ticket, but simply absorb Gerry with them on to the train. As the Florida Special pulls out, Tom stands helplessly behind the barrier, and Claudette Colbert's face seems to say 'Just *what* have I got myself mixed up in?'

The millionaires of the Ale and Quail Club don't in fact give Gerry anything, aside from a pair of oversize pyjamas, and of course

The hunting dogs; 'Sweet Adeline'; the ticket inspection

the pleasure of their company on the ride south. They adore her, naturally, and cluster round her bunk and sing 'Sweet Adeline', 'Goodnight, Ladies' and 'Merrily We Roll Along', but then they revert to form and cannot resist loosing off their weapons, and that spoils everything. 'I see we got the Club again, Ed,' the Pullman conductor observes darkly to the train conductor at Penn Station. 'You're telling me,' the train conductor rejoins, 'just let 'em try and start somethin' …'

What actually happens in the imperishable comic scenes with the Ale and Quail Club? Well, not a great deal, when you come right down to it; and separated out, the individual comic moments don't seem to add up to very much, on paper at least. The millionaires dance with Gerry in their private car; the conductor arrives and there's some broad business with a cascading sheaf of tickets; William Demarest tries to pick a fight with the conductor; the President hiccups and his detachable collar springs up; and there's a certain amount of club procedure ('Those in favour, say Aye!' and that sort of thing); after which there's the shoot-up in the bar, which we discuss in the next section, followed by Gerry's flight into the public carriage; the intervention of the conductor and his men and the uncoupling of the Ale and Quail Club's carriage. It's all over, practically, before it's begun. Remember, as a child, standing in the surf and being hit by a very large wave?

What makes the 'rich millionaires' so memorable is not that they are clearly delineated, like the Wienie King, but that they are a swirling amalgam: a glimpse of feathered hat here, a game bag there, the dogs pulling on their leashes, a passing shot of the lugubrious features of Robert Greig. They are so funny, in a sense, because they sweep by so fast and furiously: Sturges somehow makes us imagine more than we've actually seen. They have a past. They've been on the train before, with, as the conductor intimates, dreadful consequences. They are going to Savannah to shoot quail, these elderly gentlemen, all of different shapes and sizes, none of them particularly warlike, except perhaps Bill Demarest: a class of rambunctious six-year-olds who *know* that teacher has lost control.

. . . .

The Wienie King's gift enabled Gerry to pay her debts and thus depart for Palm Beach with a clear conscience. Having been swept along by the Ale and Quail Club, Gerry must now find the means to fulfil her mission

– to secure the ninety-nine thousand dollars for Tom's prototype airport – and again fate takes a hand, although this time it is Gerry who, as it were, wanders into the billionaire's bedroom, or rather steps on the billionaire's face and breaks his pince-nez. Some of Sturges' very best comic scenes are not burdened with complex originality. In the film's opening scene, for instance, the Manager repeats the words 'of course' four times, and Sturges gets a satisfactory laugh from the fourth reply. At this juncture, Gerry twice succeeds in crunching John D.'s pince-nez, and the dogs top the gag on the third occasion – and then top that by leaving John D. with a bone … *and* fleas.

Nothing is clearly defined about the 'rich millionaires' of the Ale and Quail Club. Who are they? Where did they come from? They made their money every which way, it seems.

MR ASWELD. You can be our mascot … you must be our mascot …
GERRY (*to the gateman*). Do you think it's all right?
THE GATEMAN. All right? … It's perfect.
GERRY (*to the gentlemen*). Then, thank you for your chivalry, gentlemen; I accept with pleasure.
MR McKEEWIE (*bowing*). The pleasure is ours … this is Asweld of Aswaldocan … Mr Hinch, you've heard of Hinch's Emulsion I presume … and I am McKeewie of the Seventh National.
GERRY. And I am Mrs Thomas Jeffers, alias Geraldine.
THE THREE GENTLEMEN (*delightedly*). Geraldine!

McKeewie the banker and Hinch the paint manufacturer, that's clear enough. But *Aswaldocan*? What exotic tinned fruit is this? And what august corporate boards could flap-eared Rosco Ates or that old Keystone Kop Chester Conklin possibly have chaired?

The precisely delineated John D. Hackensacker III, however, is something else altogether. He's inherited his wealth and, unlike his sister Maude, a rapacious manhunter, seems happy just to let things tick along. He has an office to go to, but doesn't actually seem to do much there. He has a yacht, but it's rather a nuisance: things tend to blow about on deck. He doesn't believe in 'staterooms' on trains, or in tipping. They are both, it seems, 'un-American'. He keeps a note of every little thing he buys, but not for any reason other than habit – and because his grandfather did the same. He is bland and mild-mannered (and let's face it, emotionally underdeveloped), and even when he's purposeful, as when ordering the two 75c. breakfasts, he rather spoils the effect by overdoing the emphasis. One imagines that no one has ever crossed him, or – apart from his merciless sister – teased him, and as a result he is ridiculously po-faced and serious. He's not unlikeable, though, in his good-natured sincerity. An innocent from head to toe. Sturges had a very particular fondness for naivety – Hackensacker being one of his most completely rounded creations, and one equalled in innocence only perhaps by Eddie Bracken's sublime Norval Jones, Trudy's substitute husband in *The Miracle of Morgan's Creek*.

....

While I was writing the above, Ted Turner, the founder of Cable News Network and vice chairman of Time Warner, announced that he was going to give $1 billion to the United Nations, the gift to be spread over a number of years. 'I'm putting every rich person in the world on notice,' he said, 'that they're going to hear from me about giving money.' 'Turner isn't the first American to get into power charity-giving,' the veteran economics journalist Victor Keegan commented in the *Guardian* (23 September 1997), 'Andrew Carnegie and John D. Rockefeller both gave away the equivalent of $5 billion at today's prices – but he is the first to turn it into a proselytising crusade.'

One cannot, somehow, imagine any of Preston's fictional millionaires on a proselytising crusade. They're all too human, and, with the exception of the Princess Centimillia, they're all notably gentle creatures. Certainly the members of the Ale and Quail Club and John D. are characterised by their unworldliness, their childishness, almost. 'This is great fun,' John D. tells Gerry in the department store after buying the ruby bracelet, 'I've never bought things for a girl before … I mean in any such quantities.' 'You have been denying yourself one of zee basic pleasures of life,' the Frenchified saleslady tells him. 'I guess I have,' he replies.

When Sturges first went to Hollywood to work for Carl Laemmle's Universal, he allowed his friends Charles Abramson and Jack Gilchrist, who were both suffering hard times, to stay at his apartment on East 54th Street, New York, rent free.[15] Once established in California, where he was living with Gilchrist's wife Bianca, and earning $1,000 a week as a rewrite man, Preston regularly sent money to

3 ~~Corsets~~ Girdles 30.

3 Brassieres (fancy) 24.6°

1 Doz. Pants (fancy) 60.00

6 nightgowns   150.00

1 Bathrobe   49.95

2 Doz. Handkerchiefs 36.00

his friends back East. The cheques were 'not loans but presents', he wrote in November 1932. 'When your ship comes in and you get very rich, you can pay me back or rather make me presents of equal amounts.'

4

. . . .

INVISIBILITY

In terms of its tightly woven screenplay, its pace, the way in which the dead straight characters are set against the ridiculous ones, the sparkle of its dialogue, the devil-may-care manner in which it happily slips in pratfalls (Toto's sudden, totally unexpected disappearance on the steps to the quay and his marvellous slow-motion deadfall from the Princess's car), and the naive devices of silent comedy (a revolving window clunks Tom on the head as he tries to prevent Gerry's flight), its eruptions of unadulterated exuberance ('You can't have a posse without the dogs') … *The Palm Beach Story* can hardly be faulted, and even its talkative passages, between Tom and Gerry (in almost all their scenes), and between Gerry and John D. on board the yacht, seem somehow less talkative and more apposite on the second or third, or even the fifth viewing. Like a Feydeau farce, the movie covers all the corners, and leaves no dangling wisps of plot – even the baffling credit sequence is logically (if totally implausibly) justified as the trap snaps shut in what must be one of the speediest wrap-up scenes in the history of the cinema.

And yet, fifty-five years on, there is one aspect of *The Palm Beach Story* which strikes, it must be said, a discordant and profoundly unappealing note: the portrayal of the 'coloured' characters, as the title list tags them – Snowflake, the bartender in the private carriage, and Charles R. Moore, the porter; the uncredited group of waiters in the dining-car; and the nameless maid who helps Gerry make herself presentable after her clothes have been left behind with the huntsmen. *The Palm Beach Story* is a remarkably sophisticated film, sophisticated, for example, about grown-up sexual relations (although an American, Sturges had the 'European' Lubitsch–Wilder touch in this regard), but it is remarkably crude, carelessly crude in the manner of the times, in its depiction of the black characters.

The sharpness, the enduring glitter of Preston Sturges' dialogue stems partly from the simple fact that even in a tiny exchange with a bit player, everyone seems to listen to what everyone else has to say, to pick up, to be alive to what is happening around them. Take, for example, the beginning of Sequence C, Scene 18, the moment when Tom hails a cop from the window of his Park Avenue apartment and prevents Gerry making an uninterrupted escape.

GERRY SITTING ON THE SUITCASE NEXT TO THE COP
GERRY. Do I look like a suitcase stealer to you?
THE COP. It isn't how you look, it's how you behave that counts in this world …
(*He taps his hand to relate the anecdote*) Now I mind the time …
(They both turn as TOM COMES INTO THE PICTURE)
GERRY. Oh, wise guy.
TOM. Thanks for holding her, officer.
THE COP. You want to prefer charges or something disagreeable like that?
TOM (*amiably*). No, I prefer not to … this is my wife, Mrs Jeffers … Mr Milligan.
THE COP. The name happens to be O'Donnell if it's all the same to you and I've got a good mind to charge you with false arrest only I don't know if I could make it stick.
GERRY. Why don't you try?
THE COP. It's too nice a morning … the heck with it … Why don't you two learn to get along together … I had to.

On one level this is a simply a workaday filler, the purpose of which is to break up (or rather momentarily halt) a chase. The character of the large slow Irish cop (J. Farrell MacDonald) is straight out of stock, and yet with his last three words, spoken as an aside as he strolls out of the frame, he is made memorable and his off-screen life becomes real.

Or consider the uniformed maid in the credit sequence, a scatty-looking beanpole, whose only function is to throw up her arms and faint, dramatically, three times, as she witnesses a series of enormities being perpetrated just off-screen. She has no lines. She's gone almost before she appears. Why is she memorable? Partly because of her height and her tottering walk, but chiefly because Sturges deliberately fixes her (the first person we see in the movie) with a singular visual gag. As Gerry departs, her long wedding train drags over the maid's insensible body

The stock Irish cop; the tottering maid; trouble at Penn Station

like a serpent slithering over a hummock. Then, in case we've forgotten her, a moment later Sturges cuts back to her, still stretched out, still in the same somehow dynamic pose.

These minor characters – the maid, the unenthusiastic prospective investor in Tom's office, the cop on the street, his brother officer at Penn Station, the staff of the Jacksonville department store – are all allowed a few seconds in the sun, a passing touch of comic humanity ('*Mister* Ha–ha–ha–ha–,' stutters the proprietor of the Jacksonville store, Julius Tannen, in an explosion of awed disbelief). They are all, however, white-skinned. The black characters are almost wholly invisible: invisible, that is, to the on-screen white folk. The white characters speak to black characters, give them orders, even on two occasions have fairly long conversations with them, but they don't listen to them, or pay attention to them, or even really give them the time of day.

In Sequence D, on board the Florida Special, after the majority of the Ale and Quail Club have trooped off to serenade Gerry, the First and Second members are discovered lounging in armchairs beside the bar in the private carriage. They're both soused. The First Member (William Demarest) is grumbling in his inimitable belligerent cock-eyed manner: they're supposed to be a gun club not a singing society. The Second Member (Jack Norton), who appears to be more refined, has a pointed moustache and a simpering voice which, it soon becomes apparent, masks a canny determination. The Second Member appears further gone than his companion until, that is, the First Member starts bang-banging at an imaginary flock of birds.

At the start of this scene there are two marginal notes in the screenplay. The First Member refers to his fellow huntsmen as 'a bunch o' sissies' and then as 'co-eds': both these mild euphemisms were reckoned too shocking for English audiences, and Sturges reminds himself to take a covering shot, substituting 'fatheads' for 'sissies' (homosexuals). This refined delicacy, even though occasioned by the Production Code, by which all studio directors had to abide, whether they liked it or not, seems incomprehensible today – just as incomprehensible, but in another register, as what follows.

The Second Member suggests that the First has missed. 'Bang bang,' says the First Member, 'I suppose I never touched 'em that time.' 'The left one got away,' observes the Second Member. 'Throw up some crackers, George,' the First Member orders the bartender (Snowflake).

Shooting imaginary birds with live shells

The racist caricature of the black servant is complete in every particular. The bartender throws up the crackers with a faintly worried 'Yassuh'. The Second Member again asserts that the First Member has missed, with both barrels this time, and is challenged to do better himself. He will – for fifty bucks. Again the crackers are tossed up. But the Second Member fires with live shells, shattering the carriage windows and then leaning back in the armchair with benign self-satisfaction. As the shoot-up develops, the bartender emerges from behind the bar: 'I wouldn't do that if I were you, gentlemen … Conductor's apt to get lil' bit irritated.'

> THE FIRST MEMBER (*threateningly*). Will you toss those crackers up?
> THE BARTENDER (*ducking very low*). Y-assuh.

Then, after another round of shots, the round-eyed, increasingly alarmed George persists with his very obvious (not to say simple-minded) warnings:

> THE BARTENDER. I wouldn't do that if I were you, gentlemen ['gents', in the screenplay] … you apt to do some damage.
> THE FIRST MEMBER (*belligerently*). Will you ['You gonna', in the screenplay] toss 'em up or am I gonna toss *you* up?
> THE BARTENDER. No sah … I mean, y-yassuh.
> (*With a shaking hand he tosses a handful of crackers in the air and ducks behind the bar*)

He warns the huntsmen a third time, slapping his hands on the bar-top like a frustrated baby, but they are too far gone in their childish contest to pay him any heed – and by now the whole club has reconvened and is blasting away. George peeps fearfully over the bar. A shot smashes the bottle behind him. He re-emerges quivering with fear, an upturned ice bucket on his head: a disposable, insignificant figure of fun – in short, a slave.

Fire at will! The camera catches Jack Norton aiming deliberately at the bartender, who is waving a flag of truce. Norton fires and hits the flag. Well, this is not quite the last we see of George. As the camera pulls away from the uncoupled carriage, a white-coated figure, left behind by his employers, jumps on to the track and runs blindly after the departing train. The scene fades before we see whether or not he has been rescued from the amiable huntsmen.

....

As Gerry flees at full tilt through the deserted dining-car to the safety of the adjoining public carriage, she passes a black cook and four or five black waiters seated at tables, taking it easy after work. She doesn't want to make a spectacle of herself before these men and slows momentarily to a walk, while at the same time pretending not to notice them.

Next morning she remonstrates with a coloured porter (Charles R. Moore) about the loss of her clothes. He politely tells her exactly what happened, and for his trouble has to absorb an insult ('[Don't just stand there saying] "No, m'am" ... You just didn't look'), racist sarcasm ('What do I go around in ... a blanket like an Indian?') and a dismissive thank-you ('I got a brown overcoat,' says the porter. 'Well, that's very kind of you ...' she replies).

When John D. and the now happily grinning porter have gathered armfuls of borrowed clothes, Gerry looks herself up and down and considers the impression she is making in a ludicrous ensemble. The

Gerry and the lady's maid

scene is not the very best in the film, but amusing enough, and a set-up for the next in which Gerry walks into the dining-car and we are treated to a daring shot of her backside, conspicuously advertised by a 'Pullman' blanket. However, it is undercut by the melancholy presence of an expressionless black lady's maid. (What service there was on those old Pullman coaches!) The maid offers Gerry her plain white earrings. Gerry doesn't say, 'That's very kind of you,' either sarcastically or politely. She says nothing and simply ignores the maid. Perhaps she has not heard the murmured offer, but look carefully as Gerry sashays into the dining-car, enjoying the turned head, and you'll see that her ensemble includes the maid's earrings.

However, having said all this, there is one exchange, between Tom and the coloured porter (Sequence F, scene 5), in which Sturges bestirs himself and gives one of his black ciphers a sense of humour, or perhaps just a sense of indignation, memorably expressed. At the West Palm Beach terminus the porter tells Tom that Gerry lost all her clothes and got off at Jacksonville.

> TOM. She got off at Jacksonville.
> THE PORTER. Yassuh.
> TOM (*swallowing*). Alone?
> THE PORTER. Well, you might practically say she was alone … the gentleman she got off wid gimme ten cents from New York to Jacksonville … ['Watch your step, lady' – as he helps a passenger down the train steps] … she's alone but she don't know it.
> TOM. Well, never mind the philosophy [an undercutting afterthought by Sturges, or perhaps Joel McCrea] … Then she's in Jacksonville.
> THE PORTER. Yessuh – Nawsir … she said that he said he was gonna take her down here on his boat, I suppose she mean yachet, but I don't see how no gentleman who can give me a dime from New York to Jacksonville can have a yachet … maybe a canoe or a bicycle … yassuh.

The trail-off of the porter's final words packs a wonderfully low-key, slightly lugubrious comic punch, and the observation 'she's alone but she don't know it' reveals a shaft of observant intelligence (not unlike Officer O'Donnell's throwaway line '… I had to') which isn't diluted by the stereotype 'yassuh … yessuh … yassuh'. Ask anyone who saw *The Palm Beach Story* a while ago, even ten years ago (and who thinks they half-remember it), what exactly they remember, and chances are they'll mention the Ale and Quail club steaming through the train singing 'A-Hunting We Will Go' and Charles Moore's pistol-shot pronunciation of yacht – 'YAT-CHET'. The Wienie King gives Tom the fare to take an 'aerio-plane' down to Palm Beach (and it gets the big laugh the second time he says the word); but for some reason it is that ludicrous 'Yat-chet' which sticks in the mind.

Sturges wrote the porter's last speech thus:

> PORTER. Nawsir … she say he takin' her down on his boat, yassuh, I suppose she mean a yachet, but I don't see where no gentleman who come up wid ten cents from New York to Jacksonville get off to have a yachet … more like a bicycle … or a canoe … yassuh.

The speech, as delivered, is of course far better. Who made the changes? Perhaps Preston spotted the inelegant repetition of the words 'ten cents'

'Well, you might practically say she was alone …'

and substituted 'a dime'. And maybe he realised '... get off to have ...' was an unspeakable phrase and recast the end of the speech accordingly. But it's a penny to a pound that it was the actor who improvised the inverted flash at the beginning, 'she said that he said he was gonna take her ...', who exercised his art, flexed his muscles and added his own touch to a corner of the canvas.

5

. . . .

THE SHADOW OF WAR

As noted earlier, despite having been written on the eve of US entry into the Second World War, and during a period of profound uncertainty for the Allies when the forces of Britain and the Soviet Union were being tested almost to the limit, *The Palm Beach Story* contained only the most subliminal references to what was occurring in the wider world of 1941–2.

On one level, from a wartime British perspective, the movie can be read as (and maybe was intended as) a straightforward antidote to the privations of war: here is an undespoiled world of millionaires and millionairesses, of sleek modern trains with staterooms and a dining carriage which offered four grades of *prix fixe* breakfast (at 35, 55 and 75 cents, or 'the very temptin' choice of the dollar ten cent breakfast'), plus an *à la carte* menu including such wonders as prairie oysters ('whatever they might be'), of yachting cruises (at the end of which 'Captain' Hackensacker makes the acquaintance of 'Captain' McGlue – not service ranks, of course), of department stores in which absolutely anything can be bought ('12 pairs of stockings – $19.98', John D. notes in his little cashbook; 'I write things down,' he says later, 'but I never add them up'), a world in which shotguns were not the reserve artillery of the Home Guard but were for the agreeable pastime of shooting game birds in Savannah, Georgia. The airport which Tom has imagined, and which is the motor of the plot, is a civil airport, to be suspended over some peaceable city untouched by Hitler's bombs (or indeed by Japanese ones). Lipstick and perfume, and even flavourful toothpaste, are in ample supply. What could be further from besieged Stalingrad or captured Singapore or blitzed London than West Palm Beach?

On the morning after the dance at the Everglades Club, John D. pays a call on the Princess who is taking breakfast in bed. Toto, dressed for polo, is in attendance.

> JOHN D. (*entering hurriedly*). Say, Maude, is this all right? (*He takes a jeweller's box out of his pocket*) You have to work fast in these matters, so I just slid down to Margetsons … and slid back with this. [(*To Toto*) Hello.]
> (*The Princess opens the box and closes one eye and rears backwards as she reveals the dazzling jewel*)
> THE PRINCESS. What is it, the Hope Blue?
> JOHN D. No, no; it's just a chip from it.
> THE PRINCESS. Boy, when you fall you fall, don't you? (*Then to Toto, who is leaning near*) Go away, Toto … this might give you ideas …
> JOHN D. (*taking the ring*). It's all right, then?
> THE PRINCESS. I think she'll know what you mean.
> JOHN D. Good. (*He starts to turn*)
> THE PRINCESS (*lifting a startling watch, chain, and pen knife from a jewellery box on her breakfast tray*). And how do you think this would look on the Captain's vest?
> JOHN D. (*departing*). Maude, you're really incorrigible. (*He leaves*)
> TOTO (*beaming happily as he sees the watch*). ! * ‡ $? + § ¿
> THE PRINCESS (*putting it away*). No, no, Toto; naughty-naughty. (*She hands him a breakfast roll instead*)

Poor Toto, the Princess's poodle, good for little except fetching and carrying. He is one of Sturges' most memorable comic supporting players, partly because he is a largely silent presence in a film filled with ricocheting dialogue – and when he does speak no one can understand him. How the Princess came by him, we shall never know. She is still married to the Prince, a foreigner, like all her previous husbands, but he has long since been cut adrift. Somewhere along the way she acquired Toto. Perhaps he was once an adequate lover, but by the time we meet him he is simply a vexed but tenacious hanger-on and, once Captain McGlue hoves into view, an extremely tiresome one. The brittle Princess is terribly rude to him, and terribly rude about him, but he doesn't mind – he's there to be abused and he knows it.

Toto, the Deauville gigolo

Toto (Sig Arno, omitted from the named players at the front of the
film, but placed fifth in the end list) seems to have an independent
existence as the Princess's hovering shadow although not really
connected to her and not really part of anything that goes on around
him: polite but not deferential, full of posturing self-confidence, his
dominant 'humour' is the dollar-sign in his eyes. He has only four words
of English: 'Hello', 'Yitz', 'Nitz' and 'Grittinks'. Just before the
exchange quoted above (Sequence H, scene 4), the Princess muses on
how to dispose of Toto: 'There must be somebody else who can use a
house guest … I can't be the only sucker in the world … Why don't you
go to Havana? … that's a nice place … and I'd treat you to a nice one-
way ticket.' At which Toto attempts his one coherent sentence in the
movie: 'Havanag … youg? … meeg? … Havanag?' 'Noug, Toto,' the
Princess replies. '*Youg* Havanag, *meeg* here.' He understands enough to
retort indignantly, 'Nitz!' On a couple of occasions, Toto gives forth in
his native tongue (gibberish) in order to express his frustration, but even
then no one pays him much note. 'What language does he speak?' Gerry
asks the Princess on their first acquaintance. 'I don't know,' she says, 'I
think it's Baluchistan, but it's impossible to tell.'

All that we know of Toto, although perhaps this is one of the
Princess's arch jokes, is that he is a refugee from his creditors, and that
he has a head for champagne. He is a sort of Deauville gigolo, attired
when we first see him like a French matelot and then later more tellingly
in an extraordinary feminine outfit which seems to be his tennis kit. He
minces, throws his head petulantly, strikes poses, is assigned such tasks
as carrying the piles of packages from the Jacksonville department store
or going back for the Princess's handkerchief. (Could he *really* ever have
mustered the energy or had the inclination to satisfy the tigerish
Princess?)

Above all, the androgynous Toto is un-American: a European
amalgam more than a native of Baluchistan; not an honest immigrant to
the United States, but a sort of rootless parasite, the absolute polar
opposite of the tall, honest, rugged, impassive Tom Jeffers (just add '-on'
to his surname, Sturges seems to be saying), an American through and
through, with an invention which will do the world a service *and* make
him rich. Well, not as rich as John D. Hackensacker III, whose
grandfather was a burglar (John D. cheerfully asserts), but rich enough.
Toto is not a caricature of a Japanese, but he speaks splenetic

gobbledygook – just like Chaplin's Great Dictator of 1941 – and the Princess even addresses him twice in German, in hopes he may do her bidding. At the Everglades Club he appears in military evening dress, with a row of medals clearly visible on the breast of his white jacket. The Princess, one suspects, bought him all his clothes, but she cannot, surely, have bought him those medals. He must once have served in some Ruritanian regiment – perhaps he may even have been a Prussian officer.

Sturges, of course, makes nothing of all this. Indeed, he even has the Princess suggest that she and Tom might drive to Fort Meyers (where she implies they could indulge in Topic 'A' – sex) and solve the problem of the ever-present Toto by putting him in the US Army. And Toto's principal function in the plot is as a broad and wholly fanciful comic foil, hovering in the background; or, as at the Everglades, licking his thumb and playing patience at the dining table, while the principals dance and get on with the all-important business of driving forward the plot. And in this Sig Arno is faultless: absently eyeing up the ladies and greeting passers-by as he trails behind the main party on the boardwalk of West Palm Beach; shooting up like a jack-in-a-box from the back seat of the Princess's car and then slowly tumbling head-first on to the ground; or bending on his polo stick in a brilliant cut-in shot at the final climax just as the truth is being revealed.

But there is also Toto the ludicrous *foreigner* – ludicrous and unforgettable. How is one to characterise an enemy in wartime, even one your country hasn't really got to grips with yet? One solution is to demonise him, with slit eyes, pebble glasses and gap teeth, or a spiked helmet and jackboots and a dripping bayonet poised over poor defenceless Mlle Belgium; another way – Preston's way, perhaps – is to laugh him off the stage.

When they are established in their suite at the Princess's mansion, Tom remonstrates with Gerry about the name she gave him on the spur of the moment. Why did it have to be *McGlue* of all names? She misremembered his mother's name – McGrew. And why, he pursues the point, make this 'McGlue' a captain? What was he a captain of – a garbage scow? Couldn't he be a captain of the last war, Gerry suggests helpfully. 'Sure, I was eleven years old when it finished,' Tom says. 'A captain in short breeches!' In what war did Toto earn his medals? In some imaginary Balkans conflict, or a campaign perhaps on the North-West Frontier near his native Baluchistan? It hardly matters. What matters is that Sig Arno made the film's first audiences laugh at this farcical un-American poseur.

No scene expresses Tom's American honesty and Toto's alien greed as succinctly as the following exchange at the Everglades, in which Tom eloquently brings the plot to its resolution – its resolution, in the sense that he makes the last move that is open to him – and Toto intimates, in the only way he knows how, that he'd like very much to be one of those foreign husbands the Princess collects and then, inevitably, must so expensively discard.

JOHN D. ... I don't know as I've I told you, Mac, but your sister and I have progressed considerably since this afternoon.

TOM. Oh, is that so. (*Now he turns to Gerry*) What's all this business about your husband wanting ninety-nine thousand dollars before he sets you free?

GERRY (*nervously*). Oh, that was just an idea that he had ... you know how people are when they get upset. I'm not sure that he actually meant it. Let's not even talk about it.

JOHN D. No, no, let's face it. Gerry naturally wants to defend this human bacterium ... Of course that's only natural and gallant ... but the fact of the matter is he asked her for it, and as soon as my name comes into it we're doomed.

THE PRINCESS. Broiled.

JOHN D. As a Hackensacker, I find it cheaper to pay than to fight. Of course ninety-nine thousand dollars isn't a small sum ... but on the other hand it isn't large.

THE PRINCESS. I should say not ... why when I think of Stefan ... to say nothing of Serge or ... that big one with the scar ... what *was* his name.

JOHN D. Itsk.

THE PRINCESS. Baron Itsk ... Lucius.

TOTO (*happily*). Itsk!

THE PRINCESS. Nitsk.

TOM. I'm awfully sorry to hear about Tom, I knew he was a failure and a dreamer, I guess, but I didn't know he was a skunk. (*He turns to John D.*) It's very kind of you to want to build the airport ... I mean the model of it ... I guess I was a little too stunned to say thank-you ... but you know how it is when

you've been waiting for something for a long time … there's only one trouble with the whole set-up … something Gerry neglected to tell you … and that is that I'm not alone in this invention … that human bacterium we were talking about, her husband, has had exactly as much to do with it as I have, so you see if you help me you'd be helping him too, you see, and I'm sure nothing could be further from your wish … I just thought you'd better understand that. (*He turns to Gerry*) How about dancing with your brother?
(*She rises without smiling and they dance away*)
TOTO (*in double talk*). ¿ # § + ?… !!!
THE PRINCESS (*without looking up*). Shut up, my brother is thinking.

6

. . . .

TRAINS, GADGETS AND PLANES

Three snapshots from the life of Preston Sturges.

. . . .

In 1907, Mary Desti and her son Preston, then aged nine, and her current lover, a Mexican composer named José Valasquez, took a train from Dresden where they had been staying with the Duncans, to Paris. They were accompanied by a cage of canaries, a parrot, three noisy dogs and a maid. Returning from a meal in the dining-car, they found their carriage, containing their tickets and money, had been uncoupled at Cologne. They themselves were en route to Berlin. At Berlin their exit from the station was barred by an official. They could not leave until they had purchased replacement tickets, refunds for which would be given after the proper procedures had been gone through. Mary threatened to call her friend the Ab-Princess of Meiningen. The official relented. Thanks to the maid's spare change they were able to spend the night at the station hotel. 'Eventually', Donald Spoto writes, 'they found their bags and animals at the Cologne train station, where a soldier with a bayonet was guarding everything while the parrot barked insults in French.'[16]

. . . .

Sturges was an inveterate and obsessive inventor. Riffling through the Sturges papers at UCLA, the film critic Geoff Brown, a rooter-out of oddities, came upon evidence of the following: 'a certain new and useful method of constructing leaf springs so that they may be very easily lubricated'; 'a certain new and useful method of attaching windows to fabric, such as windows in automobile side curtains or windows in tents'; 'a new and useful machine … which combines the advantages of the helicopter and the airplane'. There was also 'a waterproof hinge; a special method of playing *chemin de fer*; a receptacle for holding ladies' powder, a nail brush combined with a manicure bowl, and sundry other cosmetic niceties; a rowing machine exerciser, where the oars push back of their own volition, forcing the exasperated user to push them out again; a card index system for library use; a modified set of traffic lights; a gadget for making water run up a hill; a modified viewfinder for cameras; a small car with a rear engine; a vibrationless diesel for luxury yachts, such as his own; spectacles with green and red lenses for enhancing the three-dimensional effect of plays, colour film and raw nature; a hearing aid in the form of a telephone, to be called – the inventor hoped – the "Sturgephone".' Preston also devised an allegedly kissproof lipstick for Maison Desti, and – this surely was fantasy – a method of mechanically ejecting drunks from their booths at The Players.[17] One has a Méliès-like vision of the members of the Ale and Quail Club flying up towards the Moon through a balmy California night.

Most of Sturges' inventions came to nothing. He had, for instance, in the mid-1940s a notion for a chain of two hundred theatres, designed by himself and equipped with his inventions, and of course devoted to his own films. Some of the schemes and business ventures, like The Players, did become a reality and in the process used up a great deal of their progenitor's attention, time and money. One of the most enduring of Preston's ventures was the Sturges Engineering Company of Wilmington, California, which manufactured a new sort of diesel engine, bearing the Sturges name (though it was actually developed by someone else), and fulfilled a number of secret government contracts during the Second World War.

. . . .

TOM AND THE PROSPECT – IN TOM'S OFFICE
(*They are looking at a not-too-well-made miniature of Tom's suspended airport. As we watch, a plane slides down the wire and lands on the netting*)

TOM. You see, it's strong and safe, it's simple and practical, it lets the light and air through, it's practically invisible from below … [Then, having taken a phone call from Gerry, cutting her off before she can tell him the news that their debts have been settled, he goes on]
TOM. Of course this is the big one, but to build a working model in some field or a village somewhere … that small planes could actually land on to prove that it was practical … would only cost about ninety-nine thousand dollars … after that we'd be on velvet. You see it's steel mesh made of stretched cables. Every municipality, every town, every city needs one … my patent is basic …
THE PROSPECT. Ninety-nine thousand dollars is a lot of money.
TOM. Oh, but it isn't what it costs … it's what it brings you back …
THE PROSPECT (*putting on his hat*). You see I've got ninety-nine thousand dollars now, but if I was to build this thing …
TOM. Look: let's start all over again at the beginning …
THE PROSPECT. Go ahead … my time ain't worth anything … I'm retired.

[At the Everglades Club, Gerry seizes the opportunity to talk up the airport. John D. has an office, 'not that I do much in it'; perhaps Captain McGlue could come and help him …]
GERRY. That would be wonderful … you two could plan the airport together.
JOHN D. What airport is that?
GERRY. The most remarkable invention you've ever heard of … a suspended airport right in the middle of the city … you know, stretched like a tennis racket …
JOHN D. But would it be strong enough … I mean, after all, a tennis racket …
[At this point the scene cuts to Tom and the Princess on the dance floor, and the following revealing but somewhat repetitious continuation of the exchange between Gerry and John D. was cut]
GERRY. Made of steel cables, of course … about so far apart … the light and air can go through … it's almost invisible from

below … the planes can land and take off… right in the middle
of the city … isn't that wonderful?
JOHN D. (*seriously*). It's perfectly remarkable, as a matter of fact
… if those cables are strong enough.
GERRY. That's what holds up the Brooklyn Bridge.
[The film picks up the end of the exchange]
JOHN D. I might be able to help him … in fact I *will* be able to
help him … in fact I'll help him … why not?

Sturges himself dreamed up such a suspended airport in the 1920s; and,
according to Donald Spoto, 'as late as 1948 he was still petitioning the
Regional Planning Commission of Los Angeles for permission to establish
something like it for helicopters so he could have deliveries of fresh Atlantic
seafood to The Players'.[18] Sturges was not a dawdler, or a doubter like the
bored prospect in Tom's office. He couldn't understand what motivated
people to say 'no' to a project as heroic and magnificent as a latter-day
Brooklyn Bridge. Like John D., his nature impelled him to ask: 'Why not?'

7

. . . .

MARRIED LOVE

In 1942 Sir Stafford Cripps, the Lord Privy Seal and Leader of the House
of Commons, announced: 'Personal extravagance must be eliminated
altogether.' The clothes ration in Britain was cut and the petrol ration for
'pleasure motoring' reduced. Five shillings (25p) was the maximum that
could be spent on a restaurant meal.[19] *The Palm Beach Story* unfolded in
a world where none of this applied. John D. Hackensacker III turned
down the 'very temptin'' $1.10 breakfast ($1.25 in the screenplay) not to
show solidarity with his deprived cousins across the Atlantic but because
he had settled on the 75c. one which seemed to him to offer the best value
– and besides he didn't want to let any insinuating (coloured) waiter 'get
the better of him'. Cripps would have had a blue fit if he'd seen the final
bill at the Jacksonville department store. The list of goods ran to at least
three pages in John D.'s cashbook, the camera slowly running up and
down the list of extravagances.

What couldn't be rationed, of course, was sex, although it could
be censored. Words such as 'sissies' and 'co-eds' rang alarm bells in

Hollywood. To imply anyone was a sissy – and especially to imply the rich millionaires of the potentially suspect Ale and Quail fraternity were sissies (which they might well have been) – was to suggest nameless sexual practices which in Britain were still illegal and punishable by prison, and worse. Suggestions of carnal passion outside marriage raised the spectre of Taste and Decency, and on the whole were best avoided or at least side-stepped. Even the depiction of married love was problematic. Wives kissed their husbands and beaus embraced their sweethearts, to be sure, but the stopwatch was running and how often did these desperate tableaux vivants of awkward squashed-together faces really and truly convey even a shadow of authentic passion.

Gerry, however, knows a great deal about men and sex and talks about these subjects (or this subject) quite openly and frankly – and with an agreeable touch of humour.

> TOM. ... You haven't quite answered my question.
> GERRY. What question, dear?
> TOM. Why this alleged old man gave you – how much was it?
> GERRY. Seven hundred dollars.
> TOM. Seven hundred dollars ... why?
> GERRY (*innocently*). No reason.
> TOM (*sarcastically*). Is that so ... He just ... Seven hundred dollars ... (*he waves his arm*) just like that ...
> GERRY. Just like that.
> TOM (*with heavy sarcasm*). I mean, sex didn't even enter into it.
> GERRY (*surprised*). But of course it did, darling ... I don't think he would have given it to me if I had hair like excelsior and little short legs like an alligator ... sex always has *something* to do with it ... from the time you're so big ... (*she indicates*)
> TOM. I see.
> GERRY. And wondering why your girl friends' fathers are getting so arch all of a sudden ... nothing wrong, just an overture to the opera that's coming.
> TOM. I see.
> GERRY. You don't really, but from then on you get it from cops, taxi drivers, bell boys, delicatessen dealers, visiting noblemen ... [Cut from the screenplay: '... and I even think I got it from a corpse once ... at a funeral']

TOM (*exasperated*). Get what?

GERRY. You know, the look. (*She rolls her eyes and mimics*) 'How's about this evening, babe?' [Cut from the screenplay: 'Sometimes they say it and sometimes they don't, but it gives you a fine opinion of men on the whole']

TOM. So, this gent gave you the look.

GERRY. The Wienie King? At his age, darling, it was really more of a blink.

David Thomson justly described Claudette Colbert as 'a tender comedienne'. She was one of Paramount's foremost leading ladies, and not least because she could handle dialogue with intelligent ease (an invaluable gift here, in a movie fairly bursting at the seams with developed argument as well as repartee). She was born in Paris and came to New York as a girl of six, three years before the First World War. Her round, somewhat old-fashioned face was dominated by wide and beautifully expressive dark eyes. Her figure was petite, but she had about her a distinct air of determination coupled with a discreet, seductive echo of her native France. Claudette Colbert was in her mid-thirties by 1941, and although she played Gerry as a still conventionally attractive young woman, she brought to the role something more – and perhaps deep-down something more essentially attractive – a backbone of rounded maturity, and just a hint, maybe, that the leaves were turning.

I remember as a boy coming across the famous photograph of Claudette Colbert as Poppaea in DeMille's *The Sign of the Cross* (1934) – a film I'd not seen (and still haven't), but which this picture made me want to see very much – in an immense much-thumbed album crammed with black-and-white stills. She was in a bath and her palpably naked breasts floated in asses' milk. Today, the pose and the kitsch tongue-in-cheek subtext of this image seem ineffably wrong. Claudette Colbert's sex appeal in, for example, Capra's *It Happened One Night* (1934), the film for which, I guess, she's best remembered these days, was of a less obvious and far far more potent order.

The Palm Beach Story ripples with sex. Some of it is overt, some childishly innocent, some deliberately overdone – some, like the sleek modern train piling through the night towards the Everglades, may even be symbolic (although I doubt it somehow). Viewing the film now, fifty-five years on, two things strike me: the intensity of the erotic charge between Claudette Colbert and Joel McCrea in the two scenes which are the prelude to their making love (off-screen, of course); and what a lot of sexual and particularly extra-marital contraband Preston Sturges smuggled on to the screen – although in the tumultuous month after Pearl Harbor, the censor can perhaps be excused for having momentarily taken his eye off the ball.

The first sequence finds a rake-like old man, about whose habits or propensities we know nothing, inquisitively poking about on a married woman's dressing-table, spraying her atomiser (and the screenplay had him applying her lipstick too), while the woman herself (the screenplay has her in a negligee, but dawn the day and costume designer Irene put her in a shimmering wrap) spies on him, first from inside a mirrored closet and then standing in the bathtub. The Wienie King puts his head round the shower curtain to inspect the showerhead (these were more innocent days ... or were they?) and at this point, with both of them almost touching, Gerry reveals herself, and the extremely direct and knowing August–December badinage begins. The Wienie King (that name!) gives Gerry 'the look', and although she later characterises it as 'more of a blink', there are blinks and blinks, and this one although fatherly, is filled with longing, even if it is only humorous, resigned longing.

It may or may not have significance, but when Solomon Sturges finally retired, quit Chicago and came to California to spend what time remained to him near his beloved son, he brought with him his second wife, the former Marie Fulton, whom he had married in 1933, when he was nearly seventy years old. She had been Solomon's nurse. Donald Spoto records that Solomon told his son he had married Marie 'because it's more convenient traveling [with a nurse]' – adding, 'Living alone is not pleasant and I advise you to get another wife [Preston was by this time divorced from Eleanor Hutton] AND HOLD HER!'

Gerry is adopted as the mascot of the Ale and Quail Club, and although the huntsmen love her and all want to dance with her, there is no real suggestion that they all want to sleep with her (although, perhaps, in the words of John D.'s serenade, they'd like to see her in their dreams). They love Gerry, but they love her one suspects much as they love their beautifully groomed dogs. The exception is pompous Mr Hinch who takes a rather oily line with Gerry when it comes to bedtime and he has to lend her a pair of pyjamas. One feels he would have liked to take matters a step further: but he is a gentleman (he is the only member of the club to bring along his valet), so there matters must rest. The camera does not, of course, linger on Gerry as she disrobes, but it does return to her as she sits on her bunk pulling down both her stockings from inside the legs of her pyjama bottoms and stuffing them in her shoes.

The scene on the train with a genuine frisson, however, comes next. Gerry, a distressed, though not wholly irreproachable woman, runs away in the middle of the night from the distant gunfire of her would-be protectors in nothing but a pair of pyjamas belonging to a strange man (forever in danger of falling down, if they don't first trip her up), through the dining-car with its silent waiters, and into a public compartment. Here she tries valiantly to haul herself into an empty upper berth. The camera watches her agonised flailing: absolutely anything could happen as she tries and fails to pull herself up. Then from the lower berth the innocent face of John D. Hackensacker III appears (she has unwittingly kicked him in the chest), and looks up at her from between her legs – she very nearly has his head in a leg-lock with her thighs – before she steps, with a decently pyjama-covered foot, smack on his face, crunching his glasses.

> GERRY. Oh–*oh!* I'm *terribly* sorry … Oh! I hope I didn't hurt you.
> JOHN D. (*trying to blow the glass away*). That's quite all right. Just pick off any little piece you see, will you?

Compare Gerry in her pink silk wrap, peering out from behind the shower curtain at an elderly stranger licking her toothpaste, and John D. emerging from behind the curtain of his berth to find a delicate foot in his face and his cheeks and eye sockets covered in shards of glass. Both these matching (comic) scenes have a touch of illicit danger – and the second one, considerably more than a touch, as Claudette Colbert picks the glass from Rudy Vallee's face and then delicately puffs the last few little bits away. He – the actor rather than the character – can't suppress a smile as she does this.

John D.'s (comic) sado-masochistic humiliation continues. He has now put on a second pince-nez and Gerry tries again:

Breaking a stranger's glasses

JOHN D. Now, you put one foot here … (*He indicates one arm of the seat*) and one foot there … (*He indicates the other arm*) … and you'll be up in a jiffy … and I'd gladly trade berths with you but mine has already been …

GERRY. Oh! no, no, I wouldn't dream of it. You've been much too kind already. Thank you so much.

IRATE PASSENGER. Quiet!

GERRY (*putting one foot on the arm of the seat*). Is that right?

JOHN D. Well, you're standing on my hand, but otherwise it's … perfect.

GERRY (*getting down*). Oh, I'm so sorry.

JOHN D. (*shaking his hand*). Don't mention it … you're as light as a feather.

GERRY. Thank you. Good night.

JOHN D. Good night.

(*She puts one foot on one arm, the other foot on the other*)

JOHN D. One there … one over there … heave-ho!

(*She's stuck*)

CLOSE SHOT – GERRY

GERRY. Would you mind giving my foot a little push?

CLOSE SHOT – JOHN D.

JOHN D. Why, gladly.

(*He grabs her leg in both hands and lifts it over his head*)

JOHN D. There.

(*Slowly the leg slips through his hands and the heel comes gently to rest on the pince-nez. There is a slight crunch*)

CLOSE SHOT – GERRY [ON HER KNEES, REAR VIEW] – THROUGH THE CURTAINS

GERRY. Thank you so much. (*Now she frowns*) Is there something the matter?

CLOSE SHOT – JOHN D.

(*He is shaking off the remains of his pince-nez*)

JOHN D. Nothing at all … everything is fine, thank you.

Gerry couldn't possibly have taken up John D.'s gallant offer that she crawl between the still warm sheets of his berth, and anyhow he withdraws this shocking faux pas even as he suggests it, but this does not stop the dogs. The posse follows Gerry's scent, and her scent lingers on

John D.'s person. The dogs are upon him in a second, turning round and round as dogs and lovers will, not actually between his sheets, but licking him and leaving him an immense piece of bone.

John D., it turns out, is an absolute innocent as far as sexual experience goes. His sister, and later the worldly Gerry, are convulsed when they hear that he would like to hire some children in order to see how Gerry will treat them. He wants to 'bundle' – that old New England custom of married couples sleeping with their clothes on and a bolster between them – the Princess says, and again she and Gerry fall about in fits of laughter. How *could* he – in 1942? But John D. is resolutely old-fashioned: he wears Grandfather's yachting cap and has Grandfather's habit of writing down all his expenditure in a little black book. He believes tipping and riding in private staterooms is un-American, unlike his sister who has had six husbands, all foreigners, three divorces and two annulments – and she is not too sure what her current status is with the Prince. She will marry anyone, or *anything*, John D. says (only half jokingly). Everything, but everything, has to do with sex, as far as the Princess Centimillia is concerned. She has pretty much got Tom into bed, in her mind at least, from the moment she sights him standing forlornly on the quay clutching the bunch of roses intended for Gerry.

If John D. and the Ale and Quail clubmen are sexual innocents – a delicate punctilious millionaire and a bunch of raucous, incapable drunks, respectively – the Princess Centimillia is an unvarnished caricature of nymphomania. Unlike her brother or the Ale and Quailers, she has absolutely no sense of noblesse oblige. She simply seizes what she wants; and Mary Astor with her permed wavy hair, her more than slightly strained, jangling, cut-glass voice, her cute cap at an impossibly jaunty angle – and above all her knowing eyes – has her down pat.

> CLOSE SHOT – THE PRINCESS AND TOM – DANCING
> (*She is glistening with jewels draped across her chest*)
> THE PRINCESS. You don't care for me much, do you?
> TOM. Certainly.
> THE PRINCESS. Why do you let me flop around?
> TOM (*tightening his grip a little*). I'm sorry ...
> THE PRINCESS. You will care for me, though, I grow on
> people ... like moss. (*Then to Toto who tries to cut in*) Oh,

sit down, Toto, and stop following me around. *Couche – platz –*
sitz.
TOTO. Nitz.
THE PRINCESS (*threateningly*). Yitz – Toto!

She comes on like a hurricane to Tom, taking his arm, leading him
away, fending off the doglike Toto with the ease of long experience,
unembarrassed that she is openly courting a new man while the old
one, euphemistically termed a 'house guest', is still pathetically
dancing attendance. One can't really take her seriously; she is
brittleness personified, and she talks without drawing breath, which is
just as well, since if she had, Tom would undoubtedly have pulled
himself together sufficiently to come clean about his sister's deception
– but by the time he does collect his thoughts, it is too late and he is
embroiled in the plot.

Despite her relentless sparkle and vacuity ('What's knittin',
kittens?'), the Princess does, however, come across in the scene just
quoted with the authentic, thrilling air of a dominatrix. 'Why do you let
me *flop* around?' she reprimands Tom, like a teasing schoolgirl. But she

Tom tightens his grip

means it. And for a second – as she utters the word 'flop' and gives her shoulders a little shake – one believes her. The character (and perhaps the allegedly man-eating Mary Astor, too) speaks the line as if she really means it. The artifice falls away, and a flash of sexual desire hits the spectator straight between the eyes.

When John D. pokes his head out of his berth on the train, finds it between Gerry's legs, and looks sleepily upwards to see what all the commotion is about, the action is moving at such a pace that one hardly registers this as a risqué shot. On the other hand, on the day of Gerry's flight to seek a divorce, there is no mistaking the implications of the broad sexual farce.

It is morning and Tom is dreaming in the marital bed. Gerry's side is empty, the pillow not noticeably crushed and the eiderdown still decorously in place. But from the look on Tom's face it is clear what occurred the night before. Gerry writes a farewell note and, taking a pin from the collar of her coat, accidentally jabs Tom in the backside (well, Sturges could be very obvious). She escapes and he pursues, in slippers and pyjamas, pausing only to wrap the eiderdown around him. There follows one of those marvellous Sturges pratfalls. (The director understood the peculiarly sure-fire comic potential of having characters exuberantly throw their arms out: both the fainting maid and Tom do this in the credit sequence.) Here Tom launches himself down the stairs of the duplex like an Olympic swimmer diving from the block. Halfway down the corridor he contrives to lose his pyjama bottoms. He steps out of them, catches up with Gerry outside the elevator, and begins to argue with her.

At which point a woman – the lady opera singer, perhaps, who is about to be evicted – emerges from her apartment and catches sight of Tom's rear view. She screams but is made of sterner stuff than the maid and doesn't faint away. Tom turns to apologise and as he does so the elevator doors open to reveal a mass of curious passengers. As the passengers laugh at his naked buttocks, Gerry steps in to the elevator, Tom turns back and the doors close. The chase ends with Tom haring back to his bedroom to put on some clothes the better to continue the pursuit. The shot is angled through the door, so we *almost* see Tom after he throws off his dressing-gown and pulls on his pants.

The rich comic vein of characters losing their clothes, or struggling into them or being forced to wear other people's clothes runs

Man's work

through the film. Gerry dresses in her sister's wedding gown, while Tom fights his way into a jacket on the way to the church. The best man appears actually to be doing up Tom's fly buttons at the altar. The Wienie King tells Gerry to buy a new dress, which she does, although Tom of course fails to notice it, until it is pointed out to him. Then Tom, in the sequence described above, runs about half-naked, before spilling all Gerry's underclothes over Park Avenue as he wrestles away her suitcase. Tom turns up at Penn Station with his shirt hanging out and still in his bedroom slippers. On the train Mr Hinch's pyjamas come into play; after which Gerry has to dress in the thrift-shop assortment, before being re-kitted at the department store. John D. wears his grandfather's cap for the cruise to Palm Beach. Tom arrives at the quay with an over-night bag, but – curses! – he has left his dinner jacket in New York and has to borrow one of John D.'s. And Toto's outfits are something else again: his white beret, his skirts, his huge billed cap for tennis, his polo helmet, his manly leather corset.

Amidst all this clothing mayhem and extravagance, two scenes stand out: sleepy, erotic, real, grown-up. Both centre on Gerry's inability to unzip her dress. The first occurs at the end of the New York night-out when Tom and Gerry return home – in Sturges' words 'very slightly swacked' – and the second after another night-out, as John D. serenades Gerry from the garden with 'Goodnight, Sweetheart'. Neither scene is in any way exceptional. In the 60s, English schoolboys used to swoon in the front row of the circle at the sight of the back view of some (usually continental) actress and the fumbling hands of an actor unhooking her bra. This was just about the outer limits of what the British Board of Film Censorship would permit. Twenty years earlier a married man unzipping his wife's dress (at bedtime) was as far as matters went.

Nevertheless, as Joel McCrea fiddles none too convincingly with the back of Claudette Colbert's dress (we don't of course see his hands) and a look of contentment steals over her face, and he kisses her back (clothed or unclothed we cannot tell) and comments on her racing breath, and then when she somehow slips between his knees and he turns her on her side … swacked or not, this is, indefinably, the genuine article. And as he carries her upstairs and her head rests on his shoulder and she begins to murmur sweet nothings, the tomfoolery is temporarily forgotten and the moment crystallises into something human and intimate and strangely affecting.

8

. . . .

TOM AND GERRY

'You don't have to get *rigid* about it,' Gerry tells Tom after confessing that the Wienie King gave her 'the look' – or rather 'the blink'. 'It was perfectly innocent, I assure you.' Later the Wienie King returns looking for Gerry but finds only a disconsolate Tom, whom he ridicules good-naturedly for not being able to support his wife. They soon fall to shouting and then swapping insults. 'Don't you threaten me, you big baboon,' the Wienie King says, 'I'm twicet your age and only half as big but I'm awfully mean with this shillelah …' When he learns that Tom has no money, however, he immediately relents: 'Then why didn't you say so, instead of standing there like a big stinkweed … how much do you need?' Later still, poor 'Captain McGlue', finding himself caught up in the maelstrom of Palm Beach, is seized bodily by the Princess. 'How wonderful it is to meet a silent American again,' she says looking up into his eyes, '… my husbands were all foreigners … and *such* chatterboxes. I could hardly get a word in edgeways.'

Like his illustrious near-namesake, Thomas Jeffers is a visionary inventor. Sturges saw himself as one too, but he was also perhaps sufficiently self-aware (deep down) to guess why other people, such as the sceptical prospect, might have grounds for regarding his grandiose schemes and cockamamie gadgetry somewhat differently. On the other hand, Tom Jeffers is also a bit of a stick, indeed, it might almost be said, something of a stinkweed. He stands there in scene after scene, straight upright, in his suit, a blank look on his often grumpy face, registering exasperation and bewilderment, but rarely pleasure. His stubbornness is unappealing, as it is meant to be. Joel McCrea, a tall, well-built and resolutely plain-featured, out-of-doors actor, never looked entirely comfortable in a suit, but here he simply did what was required – and can lack of charisma ever have paid more handsome dividends!

Tom isn't exactly animated, although he can certainly run, when he has to, tumbling downstairs, then shaking his head like a wet dog and picking himself up for a dash down the corridor, with the eiderdown flapping. But would he have thumped the Wienie King, who had a walking stick on his shoulder, or would he have come to blows with John D. over the improper gift of the ruby bracelet, in an honest fit of manly passion? I hardly think so. Tom is essentially a boffin encased in a private world: he wants Gerry back (when she goes), but he doesn't know exactly why. He loves her, he really does, but silently, one suspects. Once his engine starts running, once he has her on his knee and can hear her breath coming faster, he's man enough, but deep down where it matters he lacks her essential vitality, her sheer zestful determination, her restless need to be doing.

How or why, precisely, Tom Jeffers married Gerry – as Gerry says at the close, that's 'another plot entirely' – we shall never know. Did he, perhaps, think he was marrying her twin, the one bound-up in the closet? His demeanour at the opening wedding *suggests* he was party to Gerry's underhand plot, but maybe not. In the event, it seems that *Gerry* married him, not vice versa. It's hard to imagine Tom incapacitating his twin brother. What we do know for sure is the answer to the on-screen question Sturges poses at the end of the front credits – 'and they lived happily ever after … or did they?' – 'Well, *no*, not exactly …'

The enduring fascination of the relationship at the heart of *The Palm Beach Story* (and it hasn't dated in half a century) stems from our uncertainty about Tom and Gerry. Do they love each other? Have they stopped loving each other entirely, or only a little, as couples do? Do they really feel they should break up? They engage lazily in sex, at the Park Avenue duplex, but does it signify anything deeper? Or is it simply an indication that they can detach their feelings from their emotions? Gerry's reference to 'the bust-up' is made only when the film is well under way: up to this point they've come across as broke, but no more unhappy than any couple who have been married for five years, and haven't yet quite got a handle on the housekeeping.

All these questions hover in the air as the plot unfolds, and the mayhem builds, and the complications multiply, and at the same time, to keep us on our toes, Sturges mixes extravagant dollops of unreality into Tom and Gerry's personal and essentially real dilemma. For one thing, the Jeffers don't in fact appear to be at all short of money. Consider the Park Avenue duplex: chandeliers, a grand piano, Mrs Jeffers in a beautiful silk wrap, her dressing-table crowded with kissproof lipstick and the 'Secret of the Harem' – and even the 'dirt' to which the wife of the Wienie King alludes is minimal (well, non-existent, as far as one can tell). Tom may be living on the edge: the screenplay has a man arrive to dun him for the office rent, but this was cut from the movie, the point having been made already. However, when Gerry takes him out for the evening on the remaining fourteen dollars, the last of the Wienie King's munificence, he still has a serviceable dinner jacket in the closet – rather than in the pawnshop.

What did Gerry see in this dull dog, leaving aside of course that he's an unacknowledged genius? It is hard to tell: she is such an amusing, attentive, talkative, enthusiastic woman. As she pauses on the kerb for a taxi to take her to church, her feet beat a little speeded-up tattoo on the sidewalk, the effect being of a girl who just can't contain her excitement, as well as her anxiety. Five years on, she has no apparent career. While her husband is at the office, demonstrating his string and sealing-wax model airport, she's still in her dressing-gown – and not visibly concerned that they are about to be evicted, or that the manager is showing her home to prospective new tenants without any advance warning.

What riles Gerry, and what gives the plot its motive energy, is that Tom – stubborn, old-fashioned, jealous Tom – refuses point-blank to let her help him, as she knows she can, by using her wits and exercising her charm. It would make them both happy, and she sees nothing wrong or demeaning in doing this: she looks on it as a worthwhile, but also an amusing challenge. What makes Gerry Jeffers so attractive today, in 1997, when equal rights for men and women is the *sine qua non* of almost every aspect of middle-class life in the West? Well, she is prepared to do *anything* to secure Tom his money, even destroy her own happiness, and yet this is an act above all of *cheerful* self-sacrifice. Gerry has the self-confidence and style not to care about herself, even as the Florida Special pulls out of Penn Station and a look of anxiety and vulnerability crosses her face as she glances back at her husband – and who could not love her for that?

If the millionaires of *The Palm Beach Story* are a sort of upside down tribute to Preston's adoptive father Solomon Sturges, Gerry is animated by something of the spirit of the indomitable, slightly crazy Mary Desti, who was forever shooting off around Europe, following her heart, attending to the needs of the even crazier Isadora Duncan, picking up and discarding lovers (she once kept company, though mercifully not for long, with the bogus charlatan Aleister Crowley, the satanist grandiloquently styled 'The Beast'); running a sometime successful cosmetics business with branches in New York, Paris and Deauville.

Mary was perpetually strapped for cash, but always optimistic that something would turn up, which of course it usually did. Gerry is much less tiresome and trying than one imagines Preston's mother to have been; but she has her energy and unstoppability, and above all her faith in the kindness of strangers.

After Captain McGlue has made his principled speech to John D. about how he is in partnership with that human bacterium Gerry's husband and how in the circumstances he is sure John D. won't want to invest in the airport, he takes his 'sister' on to the dance floor:

GERRY. What did you have to do that for, you fat-head? Don't you ever get tired of being noble? Everything I build up for you, you knock down. I've got you the money twice already …
TOM. Look, darling …
GERRY. No, no, I don't want to listen to anything that begins with 'look, darling' so that you can get off another noble saying. Can't you ever learn to be practical? Don't you know the greatest men in the world [the founders of our country – cut] have told lies and let things be misunderstood if it was useful to them? Didn't you ever hear of a campaign promise?
TOM. The way you are is the way you have to be, honey. That's the way I am and if I'm supposed to be a flop …
GERRY. You're not going to be a flop. Nobody who's been married to me for five years is going to be a flop. You're going to get your airport if I have to build it for you myself … after I'm married.
TOM. After you're married … It's a funny thing to hear your wife say.

The scene then ends, irresolution hanging in the air. But Sturges originally had something more to say about Tom and Gerry, and in the screenplay the exchange continues:

TOM. You know how much of *that* money I'm going to touch.
GERRY. You'll never *know* whose money you're touching. Some day an old investor from Arkansas will appear, or maybe it will be a young one from New Jersey, or maybe a rich Indian or an oil man from Texas … *you'll* never know; and then you'll get

rich and successful, because you really have something on the ball, and one day you'll be driving up Fifth Avenue in a big shiny car and we'll come to a stop signal, and we'll see each other and smile a little, and then I'll say: 'You know that rich Indian who started you off to making all those millions?' and you'll frown and say: 'Yes,' and I'll say: 'Well, that was me,' and your mouth will fall open and I'll laugh at you, and then the lights will change and you'll go on straight up the avenue and I'll turn off west.

9

. . . .

VIETNAM

I first saw *The Palm Beach Story* – if memory doesn't play tricks – in a 16mm print in a large high basement room in the Carpenter Center for the Visual Arts in Cambridge, Massachusetts. I cannot remember the exact year, 1968 or 1969, I think – but in any event it was at a time dominated to the exclusion of all else, it seemed then, by the news of war. We devotees, however, sat each week in this cavernous room, every aspect of which exhaled modernity, on uncomfortable stacking-chairs, with the projector and its cake-stand reel on a table at the back, so one heard the whirr and sometimes, if the film was very long, watched the change-overs at the half time coffee break.

Before each Film Society screening, a serious young man no older than ourselves named Mike Prokosch (he was unkempt in that ageless film-buff manner) stood up and gave us 'notes' on what we were about to see. He had that peculiar earnestness of the true believer. He had seen everything and remembered everything, and although he spoke in a monotone without any oratorical flourishes he kept us transfixed. One day, we thought, perhaps we shall know as much as he does, perhaps we too shall have seen *everything*.

We knew about Godard, of course, and Truffaut, and we knew a bit about the cinema's past, about *Ivan the Terrible* and *L'Atalante* and *The Cabinet of Dr Caligari* and Dovzhenko's *Earth*, and we'd seen a good bit ourselves in that careless, unfocused way one saw movies, three times a week in the 50s and 60s – and we knew, of course, that it was traditional to stand up in the tiny Brattle Street Theatre and sing along with 'The Marseillaise' in *Casablanca*. But what did we teenagers know of *The Blue Dahlia*? What did we know, until then, of Veronica Lake or Lizabeth Scott, of Joan Blondell (when young), Henry Daniell, or Barbara Stanwyck, of *Phantom Lady* and *Double Indemnity*, what of that great undiscovered American cinematic landscape before we were born, before video classics, before most everything turned up on TV – before Warren Beatty took the toothpick out of the corner of his mouth and romanced Faye Dunaway's Bonnie Parker?

And then, my friends, the maid flung up her hands and fainted, and Joel McCrea raced up the aisle and his top hat fell off, and then in tripped Claudette Colbert and gave that shy smile with her inimitable wide-open eyes, and the whole crazy business began to envelop me in a mist of pleasure … and the whirr of the projector faded, and somehow and for some still unfathomable reason nothing else seemed to matter at all.

. . . .

The Palm Beach Story belongs to that select band of comedies which can be seen again and again, and which still – always – gleam like silver sixpences in the Christmas puddings of childhood. It opened in London

in the summer of 1942, when the outcome of the war was about to be decided, and no one knew which way. The effect it had then can now only be imagined. Could it have failed to lift hearts? I hardly think so, and its reputation – always high, even when the film was out of general distribution – has never really suffered a setback. 'Nobody's perfect,' says the millionaire Joe E. Brown triumphantly at the end of *Some Like It Hot* as Jack Lemmon pulls off his wig in exasperated despair. Well, no, but this fluent, preposterous, enchanting masterpiece is for my money as near to perfection as makes no difference.

NOTES

. . . .

1 D. Spoto, *Madcap*, p. 31.
2 P. Sturges, *Preston Sturges*, p. 108.
3 D. Robinson, *Chaplin*, p. 125.
4 *Sturges*, p. 109.
5 Ibid., between pp. 64–5.
6 Ibid., pp. 109–10.
7 M. Gilbert, *The Holocaust*, p. 280.
8 *Madcap*, p. 145.
9 *Sturges*, p. 254.
10 *Madcap*, p. 80.

11 D. Jacobs, *Christmas in July*, p. 90.
12 *Sturges*, p. 255.
13 *Madcap*, p. 105.
14 Ibid., p. 113.
15 Ibid., p. 105.
16 Ibid., pp. 18–19.
17 G. Brown, 'Preston Sturges, Inventor'.
18 *Madcap*, p. 176.
19 A. J. P. Taylor, *English History*, p. 544.

CREDITS

. . . .

The Palm Beach Story

USA
1942
Production company
Paramount Pictures Inc.
UK trade show
21 July 1942
US premiere
11 December 1942
Associate Producer
Paul Jones
Directed by
Preston Sturges
Written by
Preston Sturges
**Director of Photography
(black and white)**
Victor Milner
Editor
Stuart Gilmore
Art Direction
Hans Dreier, Ernst Fegté
Miss Colbert's Gowns by
Irene
Make-up Artist
Wally Westmore
Music Score
Victor Young
Sound recording by
Harry Lindgren,
Walter Oberst
87 mins
7,876 feet

Claudette Colbert
Gerry Jeffers
Joel McCrea
Tom Jeffers
Mary Astor
the Princess Centimillia
Rudy Vallee
J. D. Hackensacker III
Sig Arno
Toto
Robert Warwick
Mr Hinch
Arthur Stuart Hull
Mr Osmond

Torben Meyer
Dr Kluck
Jimmy Conlin
Mr Asweld
Victor Potel
Mr McKeewie
William Demarest
*first member Ale and Quail
Club [Billdocker]*
Jack Norton
*second member Ale and Quail
Club [Hitchcock]*
Robert Greig
*third member Ale and Quail
Club [Mr Hinch's valet]*
Rosco Ates
*fourth member Ale and Quail
Club [Hotchkiss]*
Dewey Robinson
*fifth member Ale and Quail
Club [Featherwhite]*
Chester Conklin
*sixth member Ale and Quail
Club [Jones]*
Sheldon Jett
*seventh member Ale and
Quail Club [Kraft]*
Robert Dudley
Wienie King
Franklin Pangborn
manager
Arthur Hoyt
Pullman conductor
Alan Bridge
conductor [Ed]
Snowflake
coloured bartender [George]
Charles R. Moore
coloured porter
Frank Moran
brakeman
Harry Rosenthal
orchestra leader
Esther Howard
wife of Wienie King
(Uncredited on the print)
John Holland
best man

Howard Mitchell
man in apartment
Harry Hayden
prospect
Monte Blue
Mike, doorman
Esther Michelson
near-sighted woman
Frank Faylen
taxi driver
J. Farrell MacDonald
O'Donnell, the cop
Edward J. McNamara
officer at Penn Station
Harry Tyler
gateman at Penn Station
Wilson Benge
steward
Max Wagner
rough-looking comic
George Anderson
coloured steward
Mantan Moreland
waiter in diner
Keith Richards
shoe salesman
Julius Tannen
proprietor of store
Byron Foulger
jewellery salesman

Credits checked by
Markku Salmi.

The print of *The Palm
Beach Story* in the National
Film and Television Archive
was specially acquired for
the 360 Classic Feature
Films project from studio
negatives through Universal
International Pictures.

BIBLIOGRAPHY

Brown, Geoff. 'Preston Sturges, Inventor'. *Sight and Sound*. Autumn 1986.

Desti, Mary. *Isadora Duncan's End*. London: Victor Gollancz, 1929.

Gilbert, Martin. *The Holocaust, The Jewish Tragedy*. London: Collins, 1986.

Houston, Penelope. 'Preston Sturges'. *Sight and Sound*. Summer 1965.

Jacobs, Diane. *Christmas in July: The Life and Art of Preston Sturges*. Berkeley: University of California Press, 1992.

Robinson, David. *Chaplin: His Life and Art*. London: Collins, 1985.

Spoto, Donald. *Madcap: The Life of Preston Sturges*. Boston: Little, Brown, 1990.

Sturges, Preston. *Four More Screenplays*. Introductions by Brian Henderson. Foreword by Tom Sturges. Berkeley: University of California Press, 1995.

Sturges, Preston. *Preston Sturges*. Adapted and edited by Sandy Sturges. New York: Simon and Schuster, 1990.

Taylor, A. J. P. *English History 1914–1945*. Oxford: Clarendon Press, 1965.

Who's Who 1931. London: A. & C. Black, n.d.

ALSO PUBLISHED

· ·

If you would like further information about future BFI Film Classics or about other books on film, media and popular culture from BFI Publishing, please write to:

BFI Film Classics
BFI Publishing
21 Stephen Street
London W1P 2LN